WELCOME TO

SNOOPY'S WORLD

LAND
AND
SPACE

Based on the Characters of Charles M. Schulz

Derrydale Books
New York • Avenel

Based on the English Language Book "CHARLIE BROWN'S
'CYCLOPEDIA—VOLUMES 3, 7, 9" © 1990 United Feature Syndicate, Inc.

This 1994 edition is published by Derrydale Books,
distributed by Random House Value Publishing, Inc.,
40 Engelhard Avenue, Avenel, New Jersey 07001

Cover designed by Bill Akunevicz Jr.
Production supervised by Roméo Enriquez

Manufactured in the United States of America

Library of Congress Cataloging-in-Publication Data
Schulz, Charles M.
Land and space / Illustrated by Charles Schulz.
p.   cm.—(Snoopy's world)
First work originally published: Blast off to space. Funk and Wagnalls, 1990.
2nd work originally published: A guide to planet Earth. Funk and Wagnalls, 1990.
3rd work originally published: Our incredible universe. 1990.
ISBN 0-517-11895-5
1. Space flight—Juvenile literature. 2. Earth sciences—Juvenile literature.
3. Astronomy—Juvenile literature. [1. Space flight. 2. Earth sciences. 3. Astronomy.]
I. Schulz, Charles M. Blast off to space. 1994.
II. Schulz, Charles M. A guide to planet Earth.
III. Schulz, Charles M. Our incredible universe. 1994.
IV. Title. V. Series: Schulz, Charles M.   Snoopy's world.
TL793.S33   1994
520—dc20
94-15492
CIP   AC

10 9 8 7 6 5 4 3 2 1

INTRODUCTION

Welcome to Snoopy's World of *Land and Space*, from our own planet Earth to the planets and galaxies that make up our incredible universe. Have you ever wondered how it feels to blast off in a spacecraft, or what causes rainbows, or what the weather is like on Neptune? Charlie Brown, Snoopy, and the rest of the *Peanuts* gang are here to help you find the answers to these questions and many more about the way things work. Have fun!

ONTENTS

APOLLO SPACECRAFT

← COMMAND MODULE

← SERVICE MODULE

← LUNAR MODULE

"Eyes on the Stars"

CONTENTS

CONTENTS

CHAPTER 15

THE
MOON
UP
CLOSE

CHAPTER 13

YOUR AMAZING
UNIVERSE

CHAPTER 16

OUR MIGHTY SUN

CHAPTER 18

STAR-
GAZING

CHAPTER 14

NO PLACE
LIKE HOME

CHAPTER 17

THE FAMILY
OF THE SUN

HOME
SWEET
HOME

When you look up at the sky, what do you see? The Sun, the Moon, the stars. What mysteries lie beyond, millions and millions of miles away? Come and see different and exciting ways to travel through space. First let's learn some out-of-this-world facts about space.

OUT OF THIS WORLD

CHAPTER 1

ALL ABOUT SPACE

What is space?

Space is the huge area beyond the cushion of air that surrounds the Earth. That cushion of air is called the atmosphere. The Earth's atmosphere gets very thin at about 60 miles up. There is no air left at 150 miles high.

Can you breathe in outer space?

No. There is no air in outer space, and you need to breathe air to stay alive. Space travelers need to carry a supply of air with them.

Is there an end to space?

Scientists don't know for sure. The part of outer space among the planets is called interplanetary (in-tur-PLAN-ih-ter-ee) space. Interplanetary space spreads out for about four billion miles. It includes the Earth and the other eight planets that travel around our Sun. The space beyond the farthest planets is called deep space. That is where the stars are. A huge group of these stars is called a galaxy. All the galaxies together are called the universe.

THE ANDROMEDA GALAXY

Are there sounds in outer space?

No. Sound is created when something vibrates—shakes back and forth quickly—in the air. These movements are called sound waves. They are sent out through the air to your ears. Then you hear the sound. Outer space has no air to shake up and carry sound waves, so you cannot hear any sounds.

Huge explosions are always taking place on the Sun. If there were air all the way from the Sun to the Earth, we would hear the roar of these explosions all the time!

Is outer space hot or cold?

Most of outer space is very cold—nearly 460 degrees below zero Fahrenheit. If you could travel to the space near a star, you would be warmer. Stars are like huge furnaces. Heat streams out from them, warming up anything near them—including planets.

What can you expect to find in our solar system?

Our solar system is made up of the Sun, which is a star, as well as the Earth and the other eight planets that orbit the Sun. You'll also find asteroids, which are minor planets, and comets, which are frozen balls of gases.

Are there clouds in space?

There are clouds, but not like the ones near the Earth. Our clouds form when warm, moist air floats upward from the Earth and cools off. Some of that moisture then gathers into small water drops or bits of ice. Many of these drops of water and bits of ice together form a cloud. Most clouds are only a few miles above the ground.

In outer space, there is no water, so clouds of moisture cannot form. There are some huge clouds of gas and dust in deep space. They hide some of the distant stars from us. The clouds in space are called nebulas.

VIEW OF EARTH FROM SPACE

I OWN PROPERTY ON MARS!

Who owns outer space?

We all do! Most of the countries of the world have agreed that outer space should belong to everybody.

SPACE DANGERS: RADIATION AND METEOROIDS

What is radiation?

Scientists use the word radiation (ray-dee-AY-shun) for anything that flows outward—much like the spray of water from a garden hose. Like the water spray, radiation is made of tiny particles traveling in waves. One example of this is light streaming from the Sun or from a lamp. Another kind of radiation is heat. Heat is radiated from the Sun. Radio and television waves are sent out—or broadcast—through the air as streams of radiation. These waves are then picked up or received by our radios and TV's.

Is there radiation in outer space?

Yes, outer space is criss-crossed by many kinds of radiation. There are light waves. There are X rays, just like the ones the doctor uses to take pictures of your insides. There are other kinds of radiation, too. Radiation moves through space at about 186,000 miles per second.

NOTICE HOW WATER RADIATES FROM A GARDEN HOSE?

Is radiation dangerous?

Exposure to some kinds of radiation is dangerous on Earth and in outer space. People cannot live if the radiation hits them directly. Radiation such as ultraviolet rays from the Sun can cause cancer and other health problems. On Earth, the atmosphere protects us from some of the Sun's harmful rays.

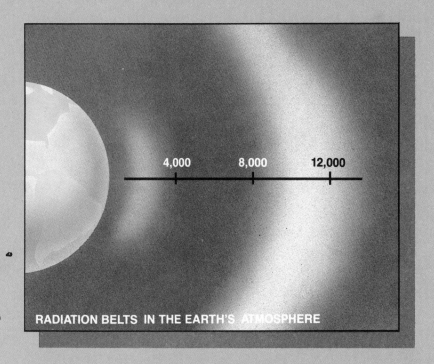

4,000   8,000   12,000

RADIATION BELTS IN THE EARTH'S ATMOSPHERE

What are radiation belts?

There are two invisible clouds around the Earth. They surround our planet like two belts looped around a ball. These clouds are called radiation belts. They are made up of tiny parts called electrons and protons—specks so small that you cannot see them, even under a microscope! Inside the belts, the radiation is weak. You would have to live within the belts for many years before any harm came to you.

What other dangers are there in space?

There are bits of rock called meteoroids (MEE-tee-uh-roidz) flying around in outer space. Many of them are no bigger than grains of sand. Some meteoroids are bits of material that never formed into planets. Some meteoroids can move hundreds of times faster than a rifle bullet. They can go so fast that even the smallest ones can do great damage to anything they hit.

A meteoroid that enters the Earth's atmosphere is called a meteor. If a meteor manages to reach the Earth's surface without burning up in the atmosphere, it is called a meteorite.

Another danger in space comes from space junk. These are the bits and pieces of material from old rockets and satellites that astronauts have left in outer space. Space junk orbits the Earth and can cause great damage to each new spacecraft that goes into orbit.

Tiny chips of paint from space junk have seriously damaged windows on our space shuttles!

CHAPTER 2

People have invented many ways to travel by air—airplanes and gliders, balloons and helicopters. All of these things can fly you around the world, but none of them can fly you out of this world and into outer space. If you want to soar through space, what you need is a rocket-powered spacecraft!

SUPER SPACECRAFT

ALL ABOUT ROCKETS

GODDARD
ROCKET

What is a rocket?

A rocket is a kind of engine, or motor, that can operate in space where there is no air. A rocket must be powerful enough to lift a very heavy spacecraft off the Earth. In order to do this, it burns special fuels.

Who made the first rocket?

Nobody knows exactly. The Chinese were using rockets more than 800 years ago. These rockets were powered by gunpowder. They were like the skyrockets that you see in Fourth of July fireworks shows.

In 1903, a Russian schoolteacher named Konstantin Tsiolkovsky (tzawl-KAWF-skee) had the idea of using rockets for flights into space. In 1926, the American scientist Robert H. Goddard sent up a rocket that went about as high as a 20-story building.

A Redstone 3 rocket launches a *Freedom* 7 capsule into space. This astronaut in training is standing in front of a Mercury capsule.

How does a rocket work?

In order for something to move in one direction, it must give a push in the opposite direction. When you row a boat, you push the water in the opposite direction from the way you want to go. When you swim in a pool, you sometimes push back against the pool wall to move yourself forward.

This kind of two-way action is what makes a rocket motor work. Fuel is burned inside the rocket. This is called "firing" the rocket. The burning fuel forms great clouds of hot gas. The heat makes the gases swell up so much that they need more room. They can escape only through an opening at the back of the rocket. Then, as the gases are forced out at the back, the spacecraft is pushed forward.

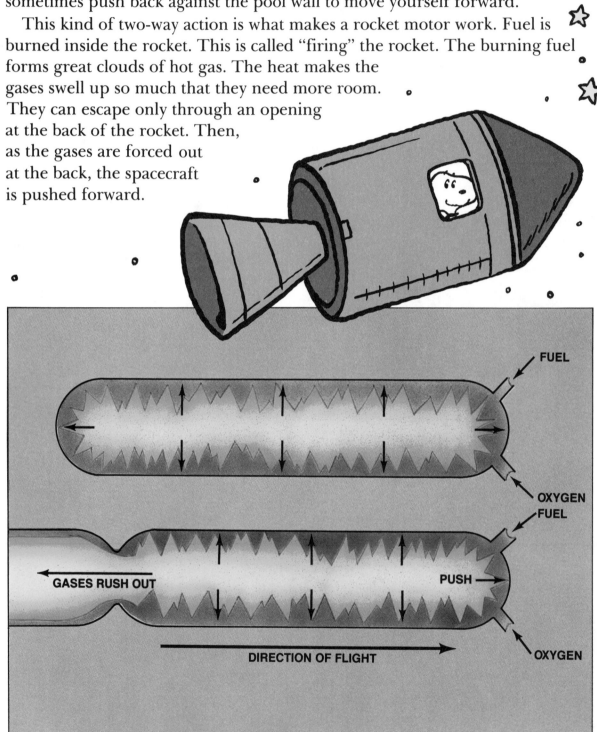

FUEL

OXYGEN

FUEL

GASES RUSH OUT

PUSH →

DIRECTION OF FLIGHT

OXYGEN

ORBITS AND GRAVITY

What is an orbit?

The path of an object around another is called an orbit. The planets move in orbits around the Sun. The Moon orbits the Earth, and a spacecraft can orbit around and around the Earth. It's just like walking around a friend.

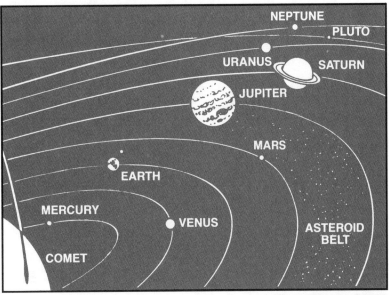

PLANETARY ORBITS

What is gravity?

Gravity is a force that every planet, star, and moon has. This force causes everything on or near the planet, star, or moon to be pulled toward its center.

The pull of the Earth's gravity holds the Moon in its orbit. The pull of the Sun's gravity keeps the planets in their orbits.

Stand on a bathroom scale. Suppose it shows you weigh 60 pounds. This means the downward pull of the Earth's gravity on your body measures 60 pounds.

How fast does a rocket need to travel to escape the Earth's gravity?

A rocket's escape speed must be 7 miles a second to get beyond the Earth's pull. That means the rocket is traveling 25,000 miles per hour!

19

How did rockets send early spacecraft into orbit?

This was done in two or three stages. Here's how a three-stage launch works.

First-stage rockets, sometimes called boosters, give the spacecraft a powerful push that lifts it from the ground. In two and a half minutes, the boosters have carried the spacecraft 40 miles. It is then going 6,000 miles an hour. At that time, the first-stage rockets stop firing and drop into the ocean.

Next, the second-stage rockets fire for six minutes. The spacecraft is now up about 100 miles, going more than 14,000 miles an hour. Then the second-stage rockets drop off.

The third-stage rockets are then fired for about two minutes. This gets the spacecraft to a height of 120 miles and a speed of about 17,500 miles an hour. The spacecraft has escaped the Earth's pull and gone into orbit around it. The third-stage rockets are left behind in outer space.

What happens to the parts of a spacecraft that are dropped off?

As a spacecraft goes up, objects such as rockets are sometimes left behind in space. The first rockets dropped are slowed down by the air. Some of these burn up as they fall. Others splash down into the ocean.

Once the spacecraft is outside the Earth's atmosphere, objects that are let loose go into orbit around the Earth. These objects are called space junk. They may orbit the Earth for a year or longer before they drop down and burn up. There are more than 3,000 pieces of space junk still in orbit.

HERE'S THE WORLD CLASS GOLF PRO SENDING A BALL INTO SPACE.

SPACECRAFT

What is the difference between a spacecraft and a spaceship?

The two words mean the same thing—any rocket-powered machine that can carry people or material into space. The word *spacecraft* is usually used in talking about a real rocket-powered craft. The word *spaceship* is used mainly in science-fiction.

How big is a spacecraft?

In the picture below you can see how large these different kinds of spacecraft are by comparing them with the size of the person. The Apollo spacecraft with its Saturn V rocket was 363 feet tall—as high as a 36-story building. It was built in 1968 and weighed more than 3,000 tons.

What kind of spacecraft did the first American astronauts use?

The first American, Alan Shepard, was sent into space in 1961 aboard a spacecraft in the Mercury program. The bell-shaped space capsule, which was less than seven feet wide, was big enough for only one person. It was pushed into space by a Redstone rocket.

What were Gemini space-craft like?

Gemini spacecraft were used in the U.S. space program from 1964 to 1966. They were similar to those used in the Mercury program, but they could carry two people. Titan II rockets pushed these ten-foot-wide capsules into space.

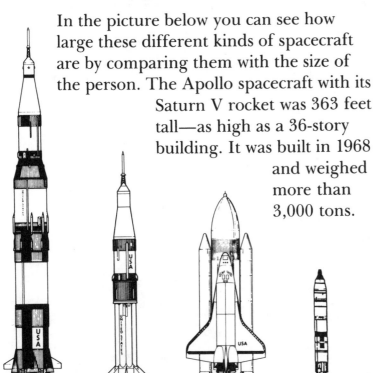
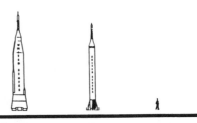

| APOLLO-SATURN V 363 FEET | APOLLO-SATURN 1B 223 FEET | SPACE SHUTTLE 184 FEET | GEMINI-TITAN II 108 FEET | MERCURY-ATLAS 95 FEET | MERCURY-REDSTONE 83 FEET | MAN 6 FEET |

What were the next American spacecraft?

After the Gemini program, astronauts began using Apollo spacecraft. The Apollo program's first test flight was made in 1967. Although this was an unmanned flight, it cleared the way for a manned launch. The Apollo spacecraft differed from earlier spacecraft. They had three main parts—the command module, the service module, and the lunar module.

What is a command module?

A command module is the front end of an Apollo spacecraft, where the astronauts lived and did their work. This module is like the cockpit of an airplane. It is sometimes called a space capsule. You can see some of these command modules at the Smithsonian Institution in Washington, D.C.

What is a service module?

A service module is the part of an Apollo spacecraft that carried tanks of oxygen for the astronauts to breathe. It also held batteries for electric power needed to supply other important necessities, such as air-conditioning, heating, and lighting.

APOLLO SPACECRAFT

COMMAND MODULE

SERVICE MODULE

LUNAR MODULE

CHARLIE BROWN REPORTING FOR BRIEFING.

What is a spaceport?

A spaceport is a place on the Earth where spacecraft stay between trips. A spacecraft is loaded, repaired, and fueled at its spaceport.

The main American spaceport is located at the Kennedy Space Center in Florida.

Like an airport, a spaceport has hangars— huge buildings used to store the spacecraft. The spaceport also has large storage tanks for rocket fuel and lots of other equipment that astronauts need to travel in space.

How is a spacecraft steered?

This is usually done by firing the rocket motors that are at the bottom of the spacecraft. To turn the spacecraft just a little, special small rockets on the sides of the spacecraft are fired. These steering rockets can be worked by the astronauts or by radio signals from the ground.

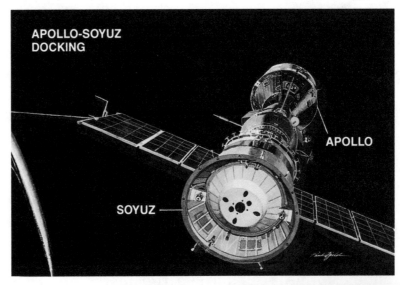

APOLLO-SOYUZ DOCKING

APOLLO

SOYUZ

Astronaut Thomas Stafford meets Cosmonaut Aleksey Leonov.

What does the "docking" of two spacecraft mean?

Two spacecraft in orbit can meet and link together. They use their small rocket motors to line up. Then they slowly move toward each other until they can lock together, or dock.

In 1975, an American Apollo spacecraft and a Soviet Soyuz (SOY-ooz) spacecraft docked 138 miles above the Earth. There were cosmonauts— Soviet astronauts—aboard the Soyuz. The astronauts and the cosmonauts visited back and forth between the two spacecraft.

23

A space shuttle can open its doors to launch satellites.

THE SPACE SHUTTLE

What is a space shuttle?

Space shuttles are the more recent of the U.S. spacecraft. A shuttle is shaped like a huge airplane and is 185 feet long. It is able to orbit the Earth and then fly back through the atmosphere and land on a runway, just like an airplane. A space shuttle can be used many times—up to 100! Shuttles can't go into interplanetary space, but they bring us one step closer to building a spacecraft that could visit Mars or Venus.

Astronauts use space shuttles to perform experiments in space. The shuttles also carry things such as communication and television satellites.

When was the first space shuttle flight?

Columbia was the first manned shuttle to travel into space. It was launched on April 12, 1981. On that first flight, the shuttle orbited the Earth for two days and performed scientific experiments.

How are the shuttles moved from place to place on the Earth?

A craft the size of a space shuttle needs a special lift! When it has to be moved from one base to another, the spacecraft is attached to a large airplane. The plane gives the shuttle a piggyback ride to its new home.

NO, I WON'T GIVE YOU A PIGGYBACK RIDE TO SCHOOL TODAY.

Shuttle *Columbia* rides piggyback.

Does a shuttle have its own rockets?

Yes. A shuttle has two rocket boosters that help it break the Earth's gravity at lift-off. After that, the rockets fall off and drop into the ocean. Special ships pick up these rocket boosters and return them to the spaceport. They will be refueled and used on another mission.

A shuttle also has on-board rocket engines. These engines help it get into space, then they guide it. They also help the shuttle return to Earth by slowing it down. Once the shuttle has slowed, gravity pulls it into the atmosphere.

How many shuttle spacecraft are there?

Since 1981, five space shuttles have been built—*Columbia, Challenger, Discovery, Atlantis,* and *Endeavour*. First launched in 1992, *Endeavour* was designed to take over the *Challenger*'s missions.

Space shuttle *Discovery* counts down to lift-off.

Why is the *Challenger* shuttle no longer flying?

In 1986, the *Challenger* shuttle exploded just after it was launched. The seven people aboard the spacecraft were killed.

One member of the *Challenger* crew was a teacher named Christa McAuliffe. She was the first teacher selected to fly in space.

25

SATELLITES

A collection
of images taken
by the *Voyager 1*
spacecraft,
during its
Saturn flyby
in November, 1980.

What is a satellite?

Anything in space that moves in an orbit is called a satellite (SAT-uh-lite).
The Earth is a satellite of the Sun. So are the other planets in our solar
system because they orbit the Sun. The Moon is a satellite of the Earth
because it orbits the Earth. Seven of the planets have satellites—or moons—
moving around them. The Earth has only 1 moon, but Jupiter has 16. Saturn
has 17! And more moons may be discovered orbiting the planets. These
moons are called natural satellites.

There are also artificial (ahr-tuh-FISH-ull) satellites. The word *artificial*
means "made by people." Artificial satellites are built on Earth and put into
orbit. Since the beginning of the space age, hundreds of artificial satellites
have been sent into space—weather satellites, TV satellites, communications
satellites, and many other kinds.

What was the first satellite to orbit the Earth?

The Moon, of course! It is the Earth's natural satellite and has been orbiting the Earth for billions of years. The first artificial satellite to orbit the Earth, *Sputnik I*, was launched by the Soviet Union in 1957. *Sputnik I* gave us information about meteoroids and radiation. A few months later, the United States sent up its own satellite, *Explorer I*. It discovered one of the radiation belts around the Earth.

What do artificial satellites do?

There are different kinds of artificial satellites. Weather satellites orbit the Earth several hundred miles up. They measure the temperature and amount of moisture, or dampness, in the air. They send back TV pictures showing where there are clouds and storms on Earth.

Communications satellites pick up electrical waves from TV stations. The waves bounce back to distant places on the Earth. That is how you get live TV broadcasts from halfway around the world. Some communications satellites are used for sending long-distance telephone calls.

Other satellites help scientists gather information about outer space. These satellites measure radiation that does not get through the air to the ground. Some scientific satellites carry telescopes that send back pictures of planets and stars.

YES, SIR. I'M SPEAKING TO YOU VIA SATELLITE.

CHAPTER 3

The word *astronaut* means "sailor among the stars." If you want to become an astronaut, you must be under 34 years old, intelligent, and in perfect health. You need to have a good education and go through a long testing and training period. Astronauts must study science and engineering and have at least 1,000 hours of experience flying jet airplanes. It takes a special person to make the grade in outer space!

THREE CHEERS FOR ASTRONAUTS

PREPARING ASTRONAUTS FOR SPACE TRAVEL

SPACE FLIGHT TRAINING

How are astronauts trained for space travel?

Scientists have set up labs on the Earth that copy the way astronauts will work, live, and feel when they are in space. For example, an astronaut is put inside a large metal ball. The ball is spun at high speed in order to put a great push on his or her body. This pressure is like the push the astronaut will feel when a spacecraft zooms upward.

Astronauts also train by moving around underwater in space suits. That helps them get used to the feeling of floating weightless—weighing in at zero pounds—in space. They also work in an exact copy of the spacecraft. In that way, they can practice using the buttons and switches that will control the spacecraft.

ASTRONAUTS IN OUTER SPACE

YURI GAGARIN

Who were the first astronauts?

The first person to fly around the Earth in outer space was a Soviet cosmonaut named Yury Gagarin (You-ree guh-GAH-rin). His flight, made in 1961, lasted a little less than two hours. Alan Shepard was the first American in space when he made a suborbital flight a few months later in his capsule, *Freedom 7*. John Glenn was the first American to orbit the Earth. His spacecraft, *Friendship 7*, circled the Earth three times during his five-hour flight, made in 1962.

Have women traveled in space?

Yes. The first woman in space was a Soviet cosmonaut named Valentina Tereshkova (val-en-TEEN-uh tay-resh-KOE-vah). She spent 71 hours in the Soviet spacecraft *Vostok 6*, which orbited the Earth in 1963.

VALENTINA TERESHKOVA

Who was the first American woman in space?

Dr. Sally Ride soared into space in a space shuttle in 1983. Americans were proud of their first woman in space. She is a top scientist and a fine athlete. Since then, other American women have traveled to outer space.

SALLY RIDE

Why do astronauts wear space suits?

Space suits keep astronauts healthy and comfortable when they take a space walk or land on the Moon. Each suit is airtight. It keeps the air, the temperature, and the pressure inside the suit as normal as possible. The astronauts also wear helmets that have a gold coating on the front. This protects them from the ultraviolet rays of the Sun. Without the Earth's atmosphere to protect them, astronauts would get sunburned very fast.

Astronauts in the spacecraft wear everyday clothes.

Can astronauts take off their space suits during a trip?

Yes, if they stay inside the craft. They must suit up again before they take a space walk or land on the Moon. If they are going far from the spacecraft, they also hook up a jet pack, which holds life-support and communications equipment. When astronauts are inside the spacecraft, they wear everyday clothes.

Why do things float around in a spacecraft?

On the Earth, gravity holds everything down. While a spacecraft is orbiting, the Earth's gravity is still pulling on everything in the craft. But another force, which comes from orbiting, also pulls on everything. The two forces are equal and cause everything—and everyone—to float. This kind of floating is called weightlessness. Anything in the spacecraft that is not held down will float around.

During a space walk in 1969, astronaut Michael Collins accidentally let go of his camera. It floated away, becoming an expensive piece of space junk!

What is a space walk?

When astronauts go outside their orbiting spacecraft, we say they are taking a space walk. Of course, they are not really walking. They are only drifting alongside the spacecraft. On early programs such as Mercury, a drifting astronaut was connected to the spacecraft by a long hose called a tether. The tether kept the astronaut from floating off into space. It had a tube that supplied the astronaut with oxygen so he could breathe, and it had electric lines for air-conditioning and radio. The space suit worn on shuttle missions today has all these things built right in!

What do astronauts eat?

Freeze-dried foods are used in flight to save space and to keep foods fresh. When food is freeze-dried, it is first frozen, then the ice that forms is taken out. The astronauts just add water to freeze-dried food, and it is ready to eat.

In an orbiting spacecraft, eating is tricky because of weightlessness. Astronauts cannot drink from an open cup because the liquid forms blobs that float around and wet anything they hit. So drinks must be kept in closed plastic bags. Astronauts must squeeze the liquid right into their mouths. Solid foods are in bite-sized pieces so that crumbs will not float around and pollute the air in the spacecraft.

On long trips in the future, astronauts may grow and harvest their own food plants in a special section of the spacecraft.

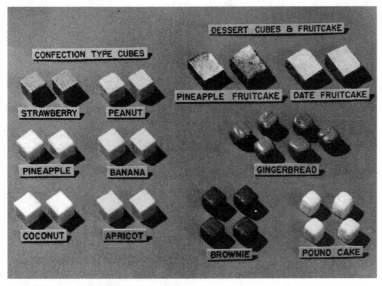

FREEZE-DRIED SPACE DESSERTS

How do astronauts get rid of body wastes?

Liquid waste is pumped into space, where it becomes a gas. Solid waste is put into plastic bags with chemicals that kill bacteria. The bags are thrown away upon return to Earth. On some space trips, all wastes are stored on board and then emptied upon return to Earth.

KEEPING ASTRONAUTS HEALTHY

What is space medicine?

It is the medical science that deals with the health of astronauts. Scientists want to know how space affects the health of space travelers. Doctors study the people being trained in labs on Earth. They also check the health of astronauts while they are in space and after they return to Earth.

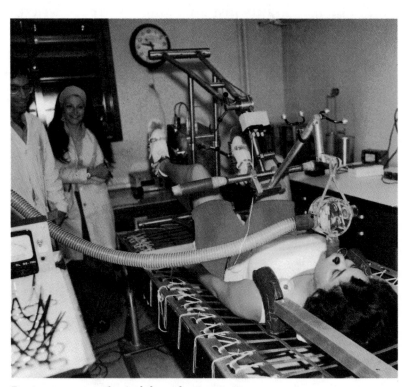
Doctors oversee the training of astronauts.

How do doctors check astronauts in space?

Electrical machines connected to the body of an astronaut check his or her breathing, heartbeat, and temperature. Readings are automatically sent back by radio to doctors on Earth.

What does space travel do to an astronaut's thoughts and feelings?

When an astronaut is alone in space for many, many days, the astronaut may become upset. He or she might even panic. Sometimes things look blurry. He or she may feel strange, and things around him or her may not seem real. However, there are always great things to keep an astronaut going. The astronaut is excited about the trip in space and knows how important the work is. Besides, the thrill of new discoveries makes space travel especially worthwhile!

CHAPTER 4

You've studied and trained. You've passed the tests. Now you're dressed in your space suit, and all systems are *go*. Where are you headed? You're about to take the trip of a lifetime. You're blasting off to outer space!

LIFT-OFF AND LANDING

NASA'S MISSION CONTROL

What is NASA?

NASA, the National Aeronautics and Space Administration, is the part of the United States Government that is in charge of exploring space. Thousands of space experts, scientists, and engineers work for NASA.

MISSION CONTROL IN HOUSTON, TEXAS

What is mission control?

All space flights are run from a center called mission control, which is located in Houston, Texas. The people in charge of the flight work at this center.

The people at mission control talk with the astronauts by radio, and they watch signal lights and special TV screens and computers to keep track of the flight.

How does NASA keep track of a traveling spacecraft?

In the past, radio signals from the spacecraft were picked up by tracking stations on the Earth. These stations were located in several places around the world.

NASA is now replacing most tracking stations with satellites that are in orbit more than 22,000 miles up. They can do the same work the ground stations did, but in addition, a space shuttle is almost always in sight of these tracking satellites. The signals from the satellites are sent into a computer at mission control, which uses the information to tell scientists where the spacecraft is.

3–2–1 BLAST OFF!

What is a countdown?

A countdown is a check-up time before a space-craft is launched from the Earth. During this time, every inch of the rocket and spacecraft is tested to see that it works. All the machinery that sets off and guides the craft is tested, too. A green light is switched on for each part that is in good working order. If something is not working, the countdown stops until that part is fixed. A person speaking over a loudspeaker at the spaceport announces how many hours and minutes of countdown are left before lift-off.

A countdown may take hours—or even days. It will continue until all the controls flash a green light. Finally, the loudspeaker booms, "10–9–8–7–6–5–4–3–2–1—ignition! We have lift-off." With a loud roar, the rockets blast off and the spacecraft begins to rise.

Why is an astronaut sometimes strapped to a seat in the spacecraft?

An astronaut is strapped to his or her seat only during lift-off and return to Earth. At those times, the astronaut's body feels a great push. It is the same kind of push that you feel when you ride in a car that makes a sudden, fast start. It seems that you are being shoved back into your seat.

The pushing forces are much, much stronger in a spacecraft that is leaving or coming back to Earth. The astronaut in a space shuttle feels a force of nearly three times his own body weight! That is why he must be supported by a seat during take-off and landing.

**3 - 2 - 1 Lift off!
A space shuttle
blasts off.**

COMING BACK TO EARTH

What is re-entry?

As a spacecraft returns from outer space, it must plunge into the air before it can land. Coming back into the Earth's atmosphere is called re-entry.

What is the heat shield on a spacecraft?

When returning spacecraft plunge back into the Earth's air, they get extremely hot from friction, a kind of rubbing and scraping of the spacecraft against the air. To protect the astronauts, the spacecraft is covered with a heat shield. Temperatures on the heat shield reach about 5,000 degrees Fahrenheit. Some of the plastic melts and burns off, taking away the dangerous heat. Inside the craft, the temperature stays at 80 degrees Fahrenheit.

A spacecraft encounters the heat of friction.

Can the astronauts talk with mission control during landing?

Astronauts and mission control talk back and forth by radio right up to the time the spacecraft comes back into the atmosphere. Then, as the heat shield begins to get hot, a strange thing happens. The air around the spacecraft becomes superheated. This is caused by friction of the spacecraft against the air. Radio waves cannot get through this superheated air. So, for several minutes, there is only silence between the astronauts and the ground.

How did manned spacecraft before space shuttles make a safe landing?

The Mercury, Gemini, and Apollo spacecraft all re-entered in much the same way. The Mercury and Gemini and the command module of the Apollo spacecraft all had thick, heavy heat shields on the rear of the spacecraft.

Before re-entry, the capsule was turned around so that the end with the heat shield faced forward. This was done by firing small steering rockets. The capsule had to enter the atmosphere tilted in a slanting path.

At the time of re-entry, the Apollo capsule could move at 25,000 miles per hour. For a safe landing, this speed had to be cut down to only a few miles an hour. About four miles above the Earth, two small parachutes were opened to slow the falling capsule. About two miles up, three big parachutes were opened. The capsule then floated to Earth at a safe speed.

APOLLO 16 SPLASHDOWN

What was a splashdown?

A splashdown was the moment a space capsule landed in the Earth's water. Astronauts used to land this way. After splashdown, ships and helicopters rushed to the floating capsule. Divers jumped into the water and placed a doughnut-shaped balloon around the capsule to make sure it did not sink. The astronauts opened a door and were lifted into a helicopter. They were then taken to a nearby ship.

Scuba divers who assisted astronauts after splashdown were called para-rescuemen.

Some Soviet cosmonauts were ejected from their spacecraft—and floated to Earth in their own parachutes! After they were ejected, retro-rockets were used to slow down the landing craft!

The Apollo capsule was tested for splashdown by being dropped into a tank of water from a tower 18 stories high!

How do the space shuttles land?

Space shuttles do not splash down in the ocean. A shuttle lands like an airplane, gliding down a runway. However, as it enters the Earth's atmosphere, it must be protected from the heat of re-entry. The outside of the craft is covered with special silicone tiles that keep it from burning up.

CHAPTER 5

After thousands of years of gazing at the Moon from the Earth, it finally happened. On July 20, 1969, an American spacecraft called *Apollo* landed there. For the first time in history, a person walked on the Moon! That person was Neil Armstrong.

TAKE A WALK ON THE MOON

THE FIRST MOON EXPLORERS

What did Neil Armstrong say when he first landed on the Moon?

"Houston, Tranquility Base here. The Eagle has landed," were the first words spoken by astronaut Neil Armstrong. We usually remember the words he said when he took the first step on the Moon: "That's one small step for a man, one giant leap for mankind."

APOLLO 11 CREW

Who were the other astronauts on the first Moon voyage?

Another Apollo astronaut, Edwin "Buzz" Aldrin, also walked on the Moon. There was a third astronaut on that flight. His name was Michael Collins. He stayed aboard the Apollo command module as it orbited the Moon.

A human footprint on the Moon.

The command modules of lunar spacecraft had more than two million working parts. An automobile has fewer than two thousand!

How long does a spacecraft take to go to the Moon and back?

The first manned flight to the Moon took about four days from the time the spacecraft left the Earth until it went into orbit around the Moon. The return trip took a little less than three days.

Astronaut David Scott salutes from the Moon.

Have there been other manned landings on the Moon?

Yes. There have been five more landings since the first one in 1969. In all, a dozen people, all Americans, have walked on the Moon.

How did the astronauts get down to the Moon's surface from their spacecraft?

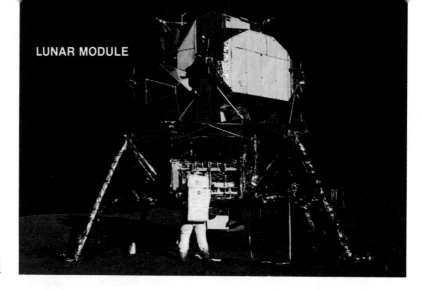

LUNAR MODULE

Two astronauts boarded a special separate spacecraft called a lunar module, which they had brought with them from Earth. Usually called the LM (pronounced LEM), the lunar module was carried into Earth's orbit attached to the third stage of the Saturn V rocket. Then it was attached to the nose of the command module for the trip to the Moon. After the spacecraft went into orbit around the Moon, the LM separated from it and was lowered to the Moon's surface. One astronaut stayed behind to operate the command module.

When the LM approached the Moon, rockets were fired to control its descent. These rockets helped the craft make a soft landing.

How did the astronauts get back to their spacecraft when they were ready to leave the Moon?

When the astronauts finished their Moon work, they climbed back into the LM and fired up its rockets. The LM flew up and met the command module that was orbiting the Moon. The two craft docked and the astronauts boarded the command module. The LM was then released. Rather than carry the heavy LM back to Earth, the astronauts left it behind. Then the rockets on the spacecraft were fired, and it headed back toward Earth.

How did the astronauts talk to each other on the Moon?

Outer space has no air to carry sound waves. Because there is no air on the Moon, there is no sound. Astronauts had to use a small radio that was built into each space suit to talk to each other. Radios can work on the Moon because radio waves can travel even where there is no air.

THERE'S A FULL EARTH TONIGHT!

GETTING AROUND ON THE MOON

Is there gravity on the Moon?

Yes. But the Moon is much smaller than the Earth, so its gravity is much weaker. The pull of gravity on the Moon is about one-sixth that of the gravity here on Earth.

If you weigh 60 pounds on Earth, you would weigh only 10 pounds on the Moon!

Apollo astronaut Edwin "Buzz" Aldrin, Jr., walks on the surface of the Moon.

Why did astronauts shuffle along instead of walk on the Moon?

The Moon's gravity does not pull as strongly as the Earth's gravity. If the astronauts had tried to walk the way they do on Earth, they would have risen a few feet off the ground with every step. They were able to keep better control and stay on the ground by just shuffling along. If astronauts on the Moon did not have to wear their heavy space suits and jet packs, they would be able to jump 35 feet high!

What did the astronauts leave on the Moon the first time they traveled there?

Neil Armstrong and Buzz Aldrin of the *Apollo 11* mission left human footprints, a U.S. flag, and a sign that read: "They came in peace for all mankind." They also left a package of scientific instruments, including a laser reflector, a solar wind experiment, and an instrument to record lunar quakes.

Athletes on the Moon would be able to leap over a two-story house. They would come down no harder than they do after a six-foot jump on Earth!

What did the astronauts bring back home?

They brought back rock samples for scientists to study. They've gathered over 100 pounds of Moon rocks!

LUNAR ROVER

How did astronauts get around on the Moon?

Some astronauts were able to ride on the Moon in style in a moon rover. The rover looks like a jeep or a dune buggy. It was specially built because the surface of the Moon is very rough and rocky. The moon rover gets its power from batteries. On one Moon expedition in 1971, astronauts David Scott and James Irwin traveled more than 17 miles in their moon rover. They explored new parts of the Moon and collected more rocks. A moon rover was used again in April 1972 by the *Apollo 16* crew. A rover was also used by the *Apollo 17* crew in December 1972.

CHAPTER 6

The next time you're outside on a clear night, take a look at the sky. How far away the Moon looks! It's hard to believe that astronauts have traveled there. Will men ever visit faraway planets? Scientists say yes!

GET SET FOR THE FUTURE

SPACE PROBES

What is a space probe?

A space probe is an un-manned vehicle launched to explore the solar system. A space probe can either fly past a moon or a planet or land on it. Probes help scientists find out about the climates and surfaces of those faraway places. Before astronauts blasted off to the Moon, scientists used space probes to discover whether the Moon's surface was hard enough to support a space-craft with people in it. And probes have told scientists that Neptune's surface swirls with stormy gases.

This space shuttle sent the *Magellan* probe (shown at top) to study Venus.

Where have space probes traveled?

Space probes have traveled millions, even billions, of miles into space. The *Pioneer 10* space probe and its twin, *Pioneer 11*, launched in 1972, were the first objects made by people to leave our solar system. During their voyages, they passed Jupiter and Saturn. *Voyager 1* and *Voyager 2* were launched in 1977. Both also flew by Jupiter and Saturn, but *Voyager 2* then went on to Uranus and Neptune before it, too, headed out of the solar system. After 12 years in space, *Voyager 2* was still sending information back to Earth!

Other probes, *Viking 1* and *Viking 2*, landed on Mars in 1976. They sent back the first photos taken from the surface of Mars.

Two space probes, called *Magellan* and *Galileo*, were launched in 1989. *Magellan* orbits Venus, measuring its atmosphere of carbon dioxide and telling us about its surface. *Galileo* is scheduled to reach Jupiter in 1995.

VISITING OTHER PLANETS

Will people ever be able to land on other planets?

Many scientists think that someday we'll be able to send astronauts to another planet. The exciting information we receive from space probes makes many people eager to visit other planets.

Which planet would astronauts visit?

Probably Mars. It's the second closest planet to Earth, and it's farther away from the Sun. It's very cold, so astronauts would have to wear special space suits to keep them warm.

Venus is the closest planet to Earth, but it's very hot there. Temperatures on the surface are higher than 800 degrees Fahrenheit. It would be hard for astronauts to live in that kind of heat.

SPACE STATIONS AND COLONIES

What is a space station?

A space station is a special kind of satellite that orbits the Earth a few hundred miles up. Astronauts live and work in it. The first American space station was *Skylab*, launched in 1973. Three different crews spent time in *Skylab*. The last crew stayed in space for almost three months and returned to Earth in 1974. While they were there, the astronauts performed many experiments. One was to take measurements of the Earth and the Sun with a giant telescope.

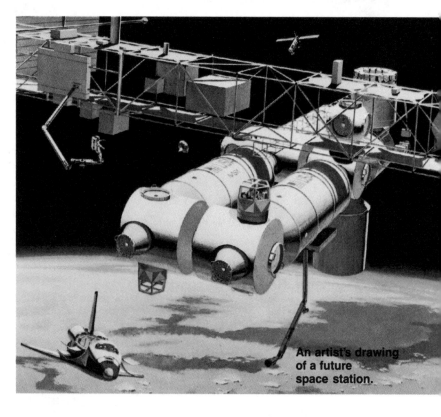

An artist's drawing of a future space station.

Skylab orbited the Earth until 1979. Its orbit weakened, and it dropped low enough into the Earth's atmosphere to burn up.

Will there be other space stations?

Yes. In 1993, the United States and Russia joined forces to build a space station that combines America's *Freedom* with Russia's *Mir*. It will be a huge joint project. Astronauts will have to build it in space—with parts brought from Earth by space shuttle.

The station will spin, or rotate, as it orbits the Earth. This motion will create a pull similar to that of Earth's gravity. With this gravity, people will be able to walk around the space station, instead of being weightless and floating.

50

What will new space stations be used for?

Scientists will use new space stations to conduct more experiments in space. American astronauts have already discovered the incredible possibilities of working in space. With zero gravity and no air in space labs, nearly perfect scientific experiments can be performed. Such experiments might help us create new drugs to cure many diseases.

A space station can also be a rest stop for astronauts before they head farther out into space. With science labs, dormitories, kitchens, and even a gym inside the space station, astronauts and scientists will be able to perform many activities.

A company that makes soft drinks has already designed a machine to sell soda in a space station!

GYM

How long can people live in space?

So far, the longest space mission took place on the Soviet space station *Mir* in 1987. Two cosmonauts spent 366 days—one day more than a year!—in space. They traveled more than a million miles during that time.

Astronauts aboard a space station perform many scientific experiments.

Will there ever be factories in space?

Yes! In space factories, we could make some things that are hard to make on Earth. For example, metals can be joined together by heating them. This is called welding. A weld is stronger if it's not touched by air while the welder is working. Welding would be easier in a factory where there is no air—on a space station orbiting the Earth.

What is a space colony?

There are no space colonies yet. But when they're built, they will be like islands in space where thousands of people can live and work. Each space colony will be different. One, designed like a huge tube about half a mile long, will orbit the Earth. Like space stations, the tube will rotate slowly to give the feeling of gravity. Large mirrors will focus the Sun's rays and provide power for electricity in the colony. Once the colony is set up, people could raise their own food in space.

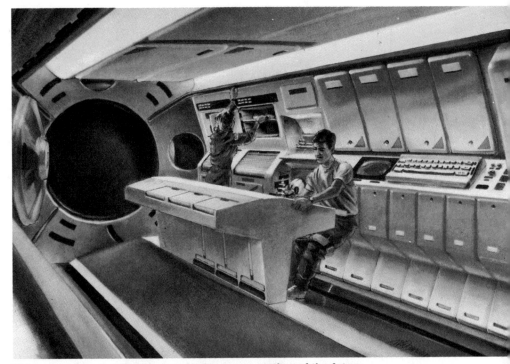

This might be a typical kitchen in the space station of the future.

Will people ever live on the Moon?

Scientists are talking about building a space station on the Moon. A lunar settlement would give astronauts a place to explore and experiment. It would also be a resting place for astronauts before they go on to visit faraway planets.

DID YOU KNOW...?

"Eyes on the Stars"

Laika the wonder dog

A dog named Laika was the first space traveler. Laika was sent up in a Soviet spacecraft in 1957, before the first humans explored space. Laika proved that living animals could survive in space.

Feeling taller?

An astronaut can grow an inch or two taller on a long space mission. Because there is no gravity in space, the bones in an astronaut's spine can move apart slightly. But when the astronaut returns to Earth, gravity will soon shrink the astronaut back to his or her normal size.

The Snoopy Space Award

NASA astronauts give out a very special prize, the Silver Snoopy medal. This award is given to people who work hard in the space program. Snoopy has been a friend to astronauts since 1969 when *Apollo 10*'s lunar module was named after him. What was the command module code-named? Charlie Brown, of course!

MANNED MISSIONS TO REMEMBER

May 5, 1961.
Alan B. Shepard be-comes the first American in space when he makes a suborbital flight for the Mercury program in his capsule, *Freedom 7*.

Astronaut Ed White takes a space walk.

John Glenn, Jr., entering the *Friendship 7*.

June 3, 1965.
Astronaut Edward H. White II takes the first American space walk. Astronaut James A. McDivitt stays in the two-man Gemini space-craft with the hatch open while White floats a short distance away. He is connected to Gemini by a tether.

February 20, 1962.
John H. Glenn, Jr., makes three full orbits of the Earth in his Mercury program cap-sule, *Friendship 7*.

December 21, 1968.
Apollo 8's three-man crew (Frank Borman, James A. Lovell, Jr., William A. Anders) becomes the first to orbit the Moon.

December 15, 1965.
Astronauts Walter M. Schirra, Jr., and Thomas P. Stafford, in the *Gemini 6-A* capsule, hold the first meeting in space! Their craft docks with another spacecraft, *Gemini 7*, piloted by Frank Borman and James A. Lovell, Jr.

July 16, 1969.
At last, men reach the Moon! *Apollo 11* lifts off on July 16, 1969, and astronauts Neil A. Armstrong and Edwin E. "Buzz" Aldrin pilot a lunar module to the surface of the Moon on July 20. They go outside in their space suits and walk on the Moon for five hours.

GEMINI 7
APOLLO 11 LIFT-OFF

July 26, 1971.
Crew members David R. Scott; Alfred M. Worden, Jr.; and James B. Irwin ride in style! *Apollo 15* is the first space mission to use the moon rover to travel on the Moon.

May 14, 1973.
Skylab is launched into orbit. It is America's first manned space station.

July 15, 1975.
American astronauts Thomas P. Stafford, Donald K. Slayton, and Vance D. Brand use their Apollo spacecraft to dock with a Soviet Soyuz craft in space.

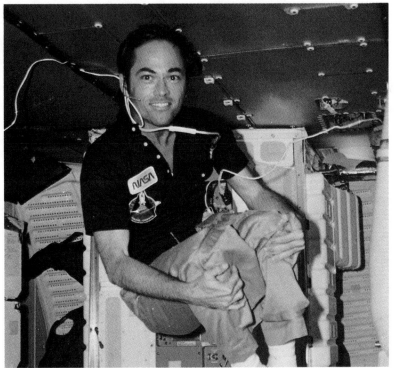

Astronaut Robert Crippen aboard the space shuttle *Columbia*.

April 1981–present.
The world's first reusable spacecraft, NASA's fleet of space shuttles, make numerous trips into space.

Hidden in the Earth's mountains, rocks, and ground are secrets to our planet's past. So get out your shovel and flashlight—it's time to go exploring. Let's discover the mysteries of our planet Earth!

THE EARTH UNDER YOUR FEET

CHAPTER 7

THE EARTH'S PAST

How was the Earth born?

Many scientists believe that more than four billion years ago, the Earth was a great spinning ball of dust and gases. Over a long period of time, the bits of dust and the gases moved closer together. Finally, they shrank and joined to become solid rock. All the movement caused by the shrinking made the Earth heat up. In fact, it got so hot that the rock melted into a gluey liquid.

After millions of years, the outer layer of the Earth, called the crust, cooled off. Because it cooled, it hardened into rock again, in the same way that melted chocolate hardens when it cools in the refrigerator. The inside of the Earth however, did not cool. It has stayed hot until today because of the great pressure at the center of the Earth. Another reason it has stayed hot is that certain minerals in the Earth give off a lot of energy and heat. Such minerals are called radioactive (ray-dee-oh-AK-tiv).

What is the Earth made of?

The Earth is a great ball of rock. Beneath its grass, soil, and oceans lie thousands of miles of rock.

If you could dig a hole deep into the Earth, here's what you would find. At first, you would see hard rock, like the kind you see above ground. The rock would feel cool when you touched it. This rock is part of the crust of the Earth.

As you went deeper, the crust would become hotter and hotter. From about 5 to 20 miles into the Earth's rock, it would be hot enough to roast you alive! In fact, scientists think that the temperature may reach as high as 1,600 degrees Fahrenheit.

If you could keep digging in spite of this heat, you would be digging in the part of the Earth called the mantle. Most of the rock here would be hard, but some would be soft and gluey—like very thick molasses. The temperature would still be rising. The center, or core, of the Earth could be as hot as 9,000 degrees Fahrenheit! Most of this core is probably liquid rock.

No one has ever been able to dig far enough to see or feel what the Earth is like deep inside. However, scientists have machines that can gather information without ever going below the ground.

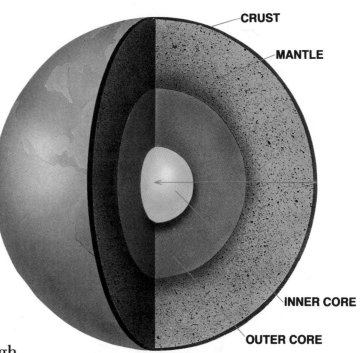

CRUST

MANTLE

INNER CORE

OUTER CORE

LAYERS OF THE EARTH

The deepest hole ever dug into the Earth went down 8 miles. To reach the center of the Earth, the hole would have to be about 4,000 miles deeper!

How were the mountains made?

Many mountains were made from rock that pushed up from the bottom of the ocean. Scientists know this because fossils of ancient sea animals are buried in the tops of the highest mountains. Fossils are the remains of plants and animals that have been buried in the Earth for many millions of years.

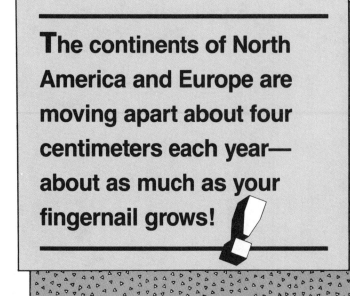

The layers of rock are squeezed into folds.

Rock is pushed up into the mountain.

Mud and sand, called sediment (SED-uh-ment), are always being carried by rivers from the land down into the oceans. Sediment that was carried to the oceans many millions of years ago came to rest in low places on the ocean floor. The skeletons of sea animals became mixed with the sediment. For hundreds of thousands of years, sediment piled up in layers on the ocean floor. The sand, mud, and skeletons got packed and squeezed together into solid rock. After many more thousands of years, forces inside the Earth squeezed the rock into folds—the way you can squeeze the skin on the back of your hand into folds. These forces pushed the folded rock upward to make many of the mountains we see today.

The continents of North America and Europe are moving apart about four centimeters each year—about as much as your fingernail grows!

AND WHEN THEY ASK YOU WHY YOU CLIMBED THIS MOUNTAIN, JUST SAY, "BECAUSE IT WAS THERE!"

(!!!?)

WELL, IF NOBODY ASKS, NOBODY ASKS..

ROCKS AND MINERALS

How many different kinds of rock are there?

There are three groups of rock. All rocks belong to one of the three groups.

The first group is called igneous (IG-nee-us) rock. This kind of rock started out as a hot liquid deep under the ground. Most igneous rock cooled and hardened underneath the Earth, but some of the liquid—lava—broke through to the Earth's surface. It flowed out from volcanoes and then hardened. One type of igneous rock, granite, is often used to make statues and buildings because it is very strong.

The second group of rock was made from sand, mud, clay, or animal and plant remains that rivers washed down from the land into the sea. It was packed down on the ocean floor in layers. Later, much of this rock rose again to make mountains. This kind of rock is called sedimentary (sed-uh-MEN-tuh-ree) rock. Cement is made from a sedimentary rock called limestone.

The third kind of rock is one that was once either igneous or sedimentary rock, but for millions of years it was bent, folded, twisted, squeezed, and heated by forces in the Earth. Because of this action, it was changed into a different kind of rock, called metamorphic (met-uh-MORE-fik) rock. The name means "rock that has been changed." The "lead" in a pencil is really graphite, which comes from a metamorphic rock.

TYPES OF ROCK

GRANITE—
Igneous

LIMESTONE—
Sedimentary

GRAPHITE—
Metamorphic

What are rocks made of?

All rocks are made of minerals. Minerals are found only in nature. They are never made by people. All of them are made of pieces called crystals. There are thousands of known minerals in the world. They have different colors, feel different to the touch, and have different strengths. If you look closely at most rocks, you will see speckles in them. These speckles are minerals.

How soft can a mineral be?

A mineral can be soft enough to be scratched with your fingernail. This means that your fingernail is harder than the mineral. Talc is one of these very soft minerals. It is so soft, in fact, that baby powder is made from it! Most minerals, however, are harder.

What is the hardest mineral?

A diamond is the hardest of all minerals. The only thing that can scratch a diamond is another diamond. Because diamonds are so rare and hard and beautiful, they are very valuable and are used to make rings and other jewelry.

This is how a diamond looks when it is mined.

64

SOIL

What is soil?

Soil is the dark brown covering over most land. It can be a few inches or a few feet thick. Some people call soil "dirt."

Soil is made mostly of tiny bits of rock. Soil also contains water, air, and pieces of plants and animals that have died. Mixed in with soil, too, are small living things such as bacteria (back-TEER-ee-uh). These living things are so tiny you need a microscope to see them.

How was soil formed?

Billions of years ago, when the Earth was young, there was no soil. Only water and rock lay on the surface of the Earth. Then rain, wind, swift rivers, and ocean waves began to pound at the rocks. Slowly, they wore the rock down, and water seeped into cracks in the rock. In cold weather, the water froze. Frozen water—ice—takes up more space than liquid water. The ice pushed against both sides of a crack and split the rock into stones. Rain and rivers washed the stones down rocky mountains, wearing them down into smaller rocks and pebbles. After millions of years, a layer of very tiny pieces of rock built up on the surface of the Earth. Pieces of dead plants and animals got mixed in with the bits of rock. This mixture is soil.

CHAPTER 8

THE EARTH IN MOTION

Although the Earth may seem quiet and still, it's full of amazing power. There are exploding volcanoes that look like the biggest Fourth of July fireworks show you could ever imagine. There are earthquakes that sometimes have the strength of a thousand bulldozers. Let's look at the many different ways the Earth is in action.

FIERY VOLCANOES

A History of the World.

Volcanoes erupted. Oceans boiled.

The universe was in a turmoil.

Then came the dog.

Does hot rock ever come out of the Earth?

Yes. Hot, liquid rock, called lava, comes out of volcanoes. Scientists give the name *volcano* to any crack in the Earth's crust from which lava flows. Lava can be up to ten times hotter than boiling water.

Scientists are not sure why a volcano becomes active, or erupts. They think that hot gases inside the Earth push lava up from below. The force of these gases may also cause the loud noise that a volcano makes when it erupts.

The Earth may shake when a volcano erupts. Fiery-hot, glowing lava, as well as steam, ashes, and even solid rocks shoot into the air. Once the lava reaches the surface of the Earth, it slowly cools and hardens. Often so much lava, rock, and ash come out that a mountain builds up around the crack. Then the whole mountain, with its crack, is called a volcano. Some volcanic mountains can take as long as ten thousand years to build up. Some have grown several hundred feet in a single day.

No volcano keeps erupting all the time. The rest period of a volcano varies from just a few minutes to several hundred years. Volcanoes that rest over many years are called dormant. When a volcano stops erupting altogether, we say it is extinct.

When the Earth heats up, hot lava and ash shoot from some volcanoes.

Are volcanoes dangerous?

Yes. The hot lava that pours out of a volcano often causes fires and can even bury a whole city. When a volcano erupts, it often sends out a cloud of poisonous gases that can kill or injure people who breathe the gases.

A Hawaiian volcano once threw out a block of stone that weighed as much as four big trucks. The stone landed half a mile away!

WHEN THE EARTH SHAKES

What is an earthquake?

Any snapping, breaking, or shifting of the Earth's crust is called an earthquake. The snapping makes the Earth shake, or quake.

Forces inside the Earth are always squeezing and straining the rock of the Earth's crust. Usually, these forces bend the rock but don't snap it, so there is no earthquake. Sometimes, however, the forces are so great that they make the rock snap. If you are close to where the rock has snapped, you feel the Earth shiver—you feel the earthquake.

Can an earthquake change the Earth's surface?

Yes. Big earthquakes can break off parts of mountains, tear open the ground, and shove huge chunks of land around. They can make buildings fall down and gas pipes burst, starting fires. Water pipes can break, so that there is no water to put out the fires. People can be killed by the falling buildings or the fire, but most earthquakes are small and do very little damage. In addition, many modern buildings are specially built to survive the shaking of an earthquake. If an earthquake does begin, don't panic. If you are inside, stand in a doorway, since doorways are strong. If you are outdoors, move away from buildings that could topple over.

SIR, THIS PLACE LOOKS LIKE IT'S BEEN HIT BY AN EARTHQUAKE!

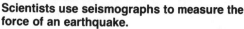

Seismograph tapes show the Earth's movement.

Scientists use seismographs to measure the force of an earthquake.

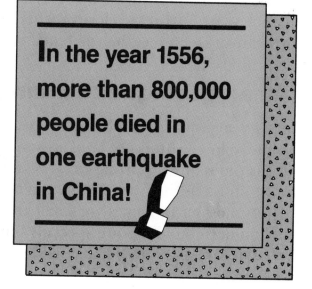

In the year 1556, more than 800,000 people died in one earthquake in China!

How do scientists measure the force of an earthquake?

Scientists have machines that measure movements in the Earth. These machines are called seismographs (SIZE-moe-graffs). The power of a quake is measured on the Richter (RIK-ter) scale. The scale starts at one. Each whole number higher means a ten-times increase in the power of the earthquake. For instance, an earthquake that measures five on the Richter scale is 10 times stronger than an earthquake that measures four, and 100 times stronger than one that measures three. An earthquake measuring two is very small and may not even be noticed. One measuring four and a half will cause some damage. An earthquake measuring six is very dangerous.

CHAPTER 9

Isn't water magical! Hold it in your hand, and it will flow out between your fingers. Put it in the freezer, and it becomes a solid block of ice! Water is a wonderful, wet, and wild part of our world.

WET AND WILD

OCEANS AND RIVERS

How many oceans are there in the world?

Even though we talk about the Atlantic Ocean, the Pacific Ocean and other oceans, there is really just one ocean. That's because each ocean is joined to the water of another ocean. The ocean has no end. You can see this if you make a small paper boat, and try sailing it around a globe. Start the boat at any point in the ocean, and keep it going in the water. Can you find a place where your boat must stop sailing? No.

How was the ocean formed?

The Earth did not always have a great ocean, as it does today. Many millions of years ago, the Earth was very hot. Some scientists believe that at that time, most of the Earth's water was trapped inside its rocks. Over a period of millions of years, the rocks began to cool and harden. As they got hard, their water came out. It ran into the low places in the Earth's crust and made the first oceans.

Other scientists think the water came from clouds that were around the Earth. As the hot Earth cooled, the clouds cooled, too. Clouds that cool form raindrops, so the clouds around the Earth rained for hundreds of years, filling the Earth's low places.

Since then, the numbers, shapes, and sizes of the oceans have changed, but oceans are still large, low areas filled with water.

IT'S ONE CONTINUOUS OCEAN!

Where is the deepest part of the ocean?

The deepest spot is the Mariana Sea Trench in the Pacific Ocean. Here the water is more than 35,820 feet deep—or nearly seven miles from the surface to the bottom. That's deep enough to swallow the highest mountain in the world—Mount Everest—which is nearly six miles high.

If you were to drop a rock the size of your head into water 36,000 feet deep, it would take the rock about an hour to reach the bottom!

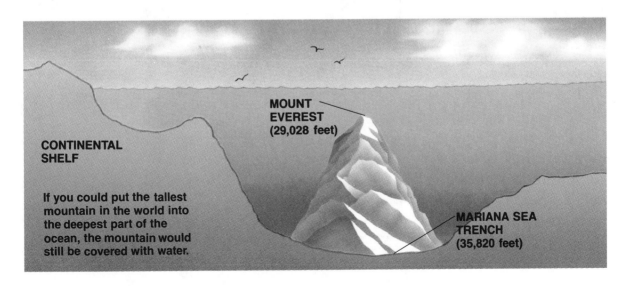

CONTINENTAL SHELF

If you could put the tallest mountain in the world into the deepest part of the ocean, the mountain would still be covered with water.

MOUNT EVEREST (29,028 feet)

MARIANA SEA TRENCH (35,820 feet)

NILE RIVER

Where do rivers come from?

Rivers start with rain. Wherever rain falls or snow melts, some water flows downhill. Water moves down toward the lowest place, carving out ditches in the ground. With every new rainfall, the water makes the ditches deeper and wider, forming streams that flow into other streams. They grow bigger and bigger until they become rivers. Rivers keep flowing along until they pour into the ocean.

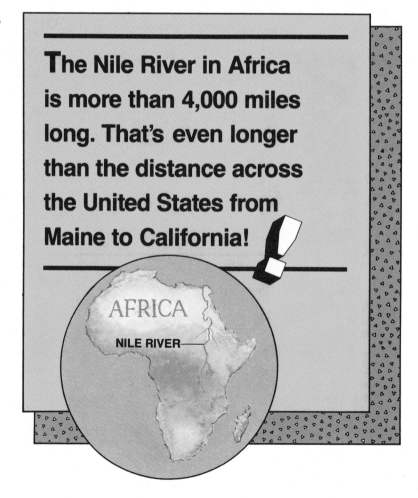

The Nile River in Africa is more than 4,000 miles long. That's even longer than the distance across the United States from Maine to California!

AFRICA

NILE RIVER

74

TIDES AND WAVES

What are tides?

Have you ever sat on a sandy beach and watched the ocean water move closer and closer to you? If you have, you were watching the tide come in. If you were still on the beach later that day, you saw the tide go out again. That means that the ocean water moved back. Once again, you could see the sand that the water had covered earlier in the day.

In most parts of the world, tides go in and out this way twice each day. They do so because the ocean water rises and falls. This rise and fall is caused by gravity—the great invisible force that all stars, planets, and moons have. The force of gravity pulls things. The gravity of the Sun and the gravity of the Moon both pull on the Earth's ocean water, causing tides. The Moon is much nearer the Earth than the Sun, so the Moon's pull on the ocean water is the stronger one. The Moon also pulls on the Earth's land, but the land is solid, so it doesn't move. Ocean water is liquid, so it moves more easily. Lakes and rivers have tides, too, but they are usually too small to be noticed.

People surf on waves like these on the coast of California.

LOOK WHAT
THE SURF
BROUGHT IN!

What makes the waves in the ocean?

Waves are ridges, or swells, of water on top of the ocean. They travel one after another across the ocean. Most waves are caused by wind blowing over the top of the water. When wind begins to blow over a smooth stretch of water, little ripples are formed. If the wind keeps blowing in the same direction, the ripples grow bigger. They get to be waves. The longer and harder the wind blows, the bigger the waves get.

What is a tidal wave?

A tidal wave has nothing to do with tides. It is a gigantic wave caused by an earthquake under the ocean. The quake pushes a part of the seafloor up or down and starts a long wave. The wave travels fast, sometimes hundreds of miles an hour. As it travels, it grows. At first, a tidal wave may be only a few feet high. By the time it reaches land, however, the tidal wave can grow to be 100 feet high. When it hits the shore, it can cause great damage. Today most scientists call a tidal wave by its Japanese name, *tsunami* (tsoo-NAH-mee).

76

FROZEN WATER

What is a glacier?

A glacier (GLAY-shur) is a huge heap of ice and snow so heavy that its own weight moves it downhill. Sometimes glaciers are called "rivers of ice." Like rivers, they keep moving downhill until they reach the ocean—unless they melt first. Glaciers move very slowly. Small ones may move only an inch or so a day. Large glaciers may move as much as ten feet a day.

Where do glaciers come from?

In some parts of the world, a lot of snow falls. If the temperature doesn't warm up, new snow piles up on top of old snow. As years go by, the growing heap of snow gets thicker and heavier. Gradually, most of it gets packed down into ice. When the heap gets very, very heavy, it begins to slide downhill. It has become a moving glacier.

As this ship moves through the water, passengers can look up at the beautiful glaciers of Alaska.

An iceberg in Baffin Bay, which separates Canada and Greenland.

What is an iceberg?

An iceberg is a mountain of ice floating in the ocean. It was once part of a glacier, but it broke off when the glacier reached the edge of the ocean.

Although an iceberg is born in a very cold place, when it floats out to a warmer area it begins to melt. The iceberg travels and melts little by little. Eventually, it gets very soft, breaks into pieces, and melts away completely. Whatever its size, most of an iceberg's ice is hidden below the surface of the water. What people see is just the tip of the ice sticking out above the water.

Some icebergs are thousands of times larger than a football field. The largest, sighted in 1956 off the coast of Antarctica, was 208 miles long and 60 miles wide!

NO, THERE AREN'T ANY ICEBERGS IN THE BIRDBATH.

CHAPTER 10

No matter where you go or what you do, weather affects your life each and every day. When summer comes and the weather is sunny and warm, you can go outside and play without a coat! When winter arrives and the cold winds blow, it's time to bundle up from head to toe. What makes weather change? The *Peanuts* gang is here to tell you.

HOW'S THE WEATHER?

Weather and Climate

What is weather?

When you talk about weather, you are really talking about the air. How hot or cold is the air? How much dampness, or moisture, is in it? How fast is the air moving? How heavily does it press on the Earth? The answers to these questions tell about the weather.

What's the difference between weather and climate?

Weather tells what the air is like in a place at any one time. Climate tells what the weather is like in general, all year round. If a place has much more dry weather than wet weather, we say it has a dry climate. If it has much more hot weather than cold weather, we say it has a hot climate. Tucson, Arizona, for example, has a hot, dry climate. On most summer, spring, and fall days in Tucson, the weather is dry, sunny, and hot. Though the temperature cools a bit in winter, Tucson's climate is still mostly sunny, dry, and hot.

Weather changes each day. Climate stays much the same one year after another, but it may change over periods of hundreds or thousands of years.

What makes climates different?

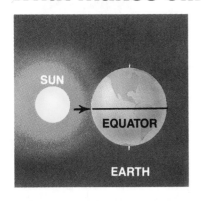

The location of a place on the Earth decides its climate. If you live close to either the North Pole or the South Pole, you live in a cold climate. The Sun's rays hit these areas at a great slant and don't warm the land very much. But if you live somewhere around the middle of the Earth—near what we call the equator (ih-KWAY-tur)—your hometown probably has a climate that is hot all year round. That is because the Sun's rays hit this area fairly directly. The more directly the Sun's rays hit a place, the warmer that place is. If you live near the equator, your hometown not only gets more Sun, but it also gets more rain than places very far north or south.

How high up you live also makes a difference in the climate. In the mountains, you are likely to have a cooler climate than at a lower level.

If you live near the ocean, your winters are warmer and your summers cooler than those in places far from the ocean. Your town usually has more rain than inland places, too. Winds and the movement of water in the ocean near your home also help to make your climate the way it is.

FORECASTING THE WEATHER

How do weather forecasters know what tomorrow's weather will be?

Tomorrow's weather is already forming in the air above the Earth. Weather forecasters get reports from many thousands of weather stations on what is happening to the air all around the world. These stations measure the temperature and the amount of rain or snow that falls. They also measure how much moisture the air holds, and how fast the weather is carried by planetary (PLAN-ih-tair-ee) winds—winds that blow all the time over large areas of the Earth. Airlines and ships at sea send radio messages every few hours about the weather where they are. Cameras and other kinds of equipment circle the Earth in weather satellites, sending back pictures and other information. All these facts are put together on special maps that show what kind of weather is heading your way.

AH! ACCORDING TO THE WEATHER FORECAST, I'LL HAVE CLEAR SKIES ALL WEEK.

What do forecasters mean when they say the barometer is rising?

In a weather report, the weather forecaster may say that the barometer (buh-ROM-uh-tur) is rising or falling. A barometer is a special instrument that measures how heavily the air is pressing on the Earth. When the barometer is rising, it means that the air is pressing harder on the Earth.

When the barometer is falling, it means the air is pressing less on the Earth.

Knowing the air pressure helps people predict the weather. When the air pressure is rising, clear skies and cool weather are probably on their way. When the air pressure is falling, stormy weather is probably in store for us.

The word *high* circled on a weather map shows the center of high air pressure. The word *low* shows the center of low air pressure.

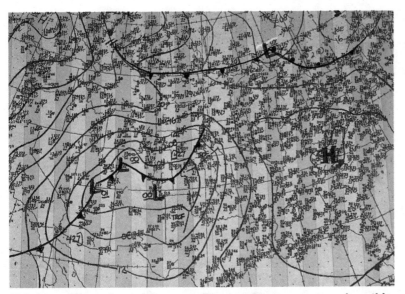

This is a picture of a weather map. Forecasters use maps such as this to tell us whether we'll have rain or sunny skies.

What do forecasters mean by humidity?

Humidity is the moisture, or water vapor, in the air. If there is a lot of water vapor in the air, the humidity is high. If there is very little water vapor in the air, the humidity is low.

What are cold fronts and warm fronts?

A large mass of air with about the same amount of moisture and temperature is called a front. A cold front is the leading edge of a cold air mass. It often brings showers and thunderstorms with fast winds. A warm front is the leading edge of a warm air mass. If often brings steady rains or snow.

CLOUDS, FOG, DEW, AND FROST

What makes a cloud?

A cloud is made up of very tiny drops of water, called cloud droplets. Air always has some water vapor in it. If the air is warm, it is light, and it rises. As it rises, it cools. Cool air cannot hold as much water vapor as warm air, so the particles of water vapor join together, or condense. They usually condense around tiny specks of dust or salt in the air and form water droplets. If the air is very cold, they form bits of ice called ice crystals. The water droplets and ice crystals are light enough to float in the air. Any one droplet or ice crystal is too small for the eye to see, but a whole crowd of them makes a cloud.

The big fluffy clouds that you see in the sky are called cumulonimbus clouds.

What is fog?

A cloud that forms close to the ground is called fog. If you walk in fog, you cannot see separate little droplets, but you can often feel them on your face. A whole crowd of droplets can make such a thick fog cloud that you cannot see through it.

What is smog?

The word *smog* is a combination of the words *smoke* and *fog*—and that's pretty much what smog is. The air always has some bits of dust floating around in it. In cities, the air also contains other particles—soot and smoke from chimneys, chemicals from factories, and fumes from automobile exhaust. We say such air is polluted. On breezy days, moving air carries the polluting particles away. On still days, a blanket of air heavy with moisture may hang over the city. Then none of the dirty particles blow away. Water droplets form around them. The dark cloud or fog they make is called smog. When you breathe in a lot of the dirty particles all at once, your lungs can be hurt. Smog is the worst kind of air pollution.

SORRY, CHUCK! I JUST COULDN'T SEE YOU IN ALL THIS FOG.

Where does dew come from?

Dew is moisture from the air that has gathered in drops on leaves and blades of grass. At night the Earth and the air near it usually cool off. So do grasses and other plants. Cool air cannot hold as much moisture as warm air can, so some of the moisture in the air condenses into drops of water on the leaves and grass. These drops are dew.

1. Heat from the Sun causes moisture from the Earth to evaporate into the warm air.

2. After sunset, the air and the Earth cool. Moisture condenses, and dewdrops form.

What is frost?

Frost is like dew. When the night is very cold, however, the moisture in the air forms ice, or frost, instead of water, or dew. Like dew, frost forms on grasses and other plants.

86

I T'S WINDY OUTSIDE!

What makes the winds blow?

The air around us is always moving. It moves because the air pressure is different in different places. When air is warmed by the sun, it gets lighter. It rises and then moves to a spot with colder air. The colder air sinks and then moves to the warm area. You feel this movement as wind.

There are two kinds of wind. One kind blows within a small area. For example, the air in a cloudy place is cooler than the air in a sunny place. The temperature difference causes the air to move, or the wind to blow.

The planetary winds are the second kind of wind. They blow all the time over large areas of the Earth. They move between cool parts of the Earth near the North Pole and South Pole and warm parts of the Earth near the equator. Planetary winds move clouds and storms from one place to another.

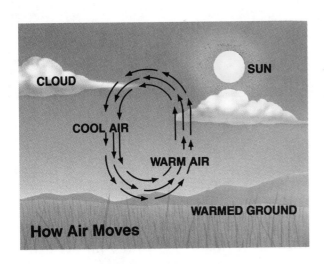

CLOUD
SUN
COOL AIR
WARM AIR
WARMED GROUND
How Air Moves

How fast is the wind?

Near the ground, winds usually blow more slowly than a car moves on a highway—less than 50 miles an hour. High up in the air, winds blow faster. Wind gusts of up to 231 miles an hour have been measured at the top of Mount Washington, in New Hampshire. That is about as fast as a race car in the Indy 500!

TORNADOES AND HURRICANES

The funnel of this tornado looks black because of all the dust it's sweeping along.

What is a tornado?

A tornado is a noisy, funnel-shaped windstorm that often sweeps across parts of the United States and western Africa. It looks like a long sleeve reaching down from a huge dark cloud. In a tornado, wind whirls around and around in a circle about the size of two or three football fields. Very little air is in the center of this circle. Like a giant vacuum cleaner, the tornado can suck up anything in its path. Up go houses, cars, animals, people, and even railroad tracks. They may come down again later, far from where the storm picked them up. That's what happened to Dorothy and her dog, Toto, in *The Wizard of Oz*. A tornado can also flatten big buildings or even make them explode.

The whirling winds of a tornado can spin as fast as 280 miles an hour, but the whole tornado, spinning like a top, moves along at 20 to 40 miles an hour—about the speed of a car traveling down a city street.

What is a hurricane?

A hurricane is a wild windstorm that starts at sea. Like a tornado, a hurricane is made up of whirling winds. Unlike a tornado, a hurricane is very large. It usually stretches across 300 or 400 miles at one time.

Inside a hurricane, the wind is whirling at speeds of from 75 to 200 miles an hour. A hurricane's wild winds cause huge waves to form on the ocean. The waves can sink ships, and the wind can tear up trees and buildings along the coast. Hurricanes usually bring heavy rains, too. These rains, as well as the high waves, can cause floods.

Eye of the storm

All of this area is getting the storm

HURRICANE OVER FLORIDA

What is the eye of the storm?

At the center of a hurricane's circle of whirling winds is a quiet space with clear skies above. This is the "eye" of a hurricane. It is usually about 20 miles across. Some people think the hurricane is over when the eye of the storm reaches them. The wind dies down, and the sky is bright above, but the whole storm circle is still traveling. In a few hours, the other side of the whirlwind will arrive, bringing more wild winds and heavy rains.

How are hurricanes named?

In the early 1900s, an Australian weatherman, Clement Wragge, began naming hurricanes after people he didn't like, particularly politicians. Now male and female names are chosen years in advance for naming future hurricanes.

I WONDER IF THERE'S EVER BEEN A "HURRICANE LUCY"?

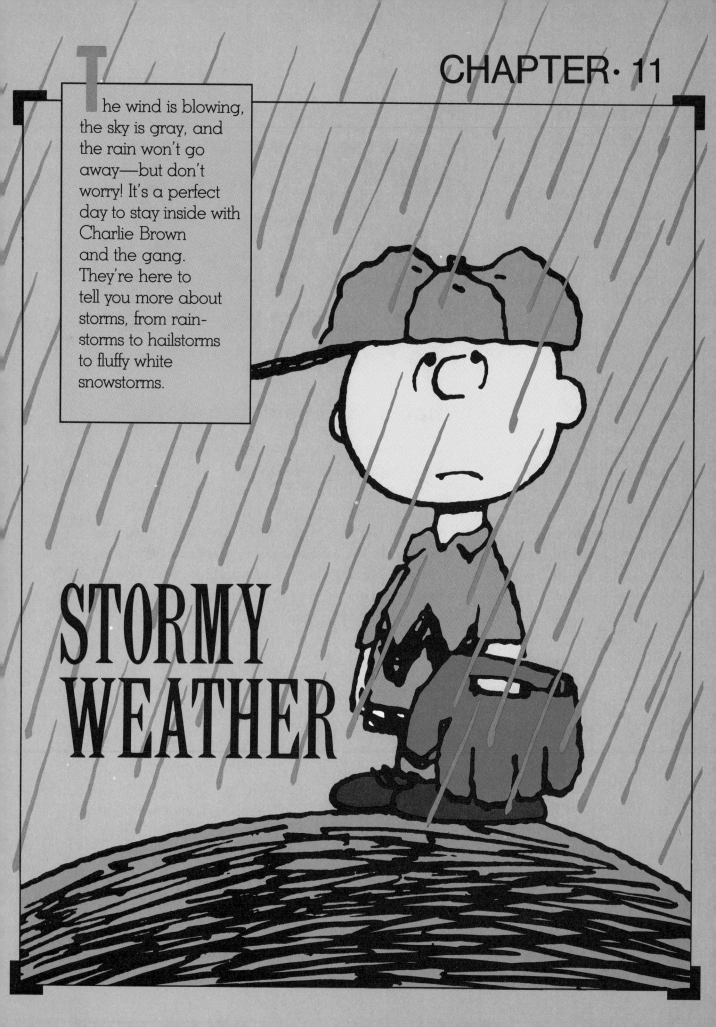

RAIN

Where does rain come from?

Rain comes from clouds. When a cloud grows big, the cloud droplets in it begin to bump into one another. They join together and form big drops. The big drops are too heavy to float in the air, so they fall to Earth as rain.

Raindrops are not tear-shaped as artists often draw them. They are perfectly round!

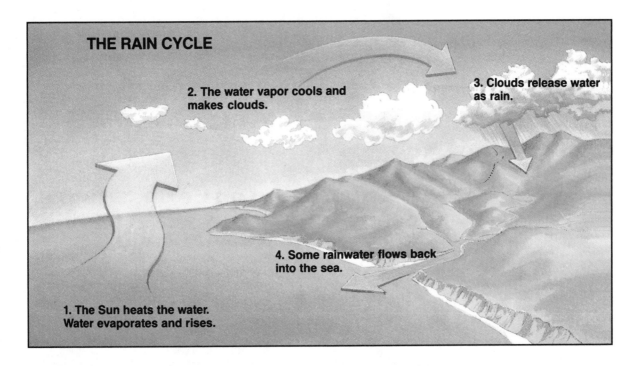

THE RAIN CYCLE

2. The water vapor cools and makes clouds.

3. Clouds release water as rain.

4. Some rainwater flows back into the sea.

1. The Sun heats the water. Water evaporates and rises.

Why are deserts so dry?

Deserts are dry because they get very little rain. Many deserts are separated from the sea by mountains. Winds that blow onto the land from the sea carry a lot of moisture. When the winds start blowing up mountain slopes, they become cooler. Cooler winds cannot hold as much moisture as warmer ones. So the cooled-off winds drop their moisture in the form of rain or snow before reaching the mountaintops. By the time the winds reach the other side of the mountains, almost no moisture is left in them. The land on the other side of the mountains gets very little rain. It can become a desert.

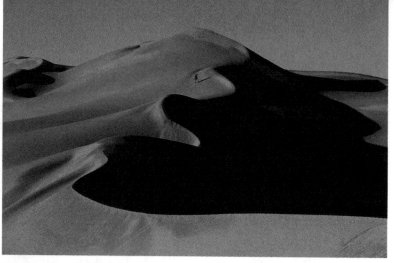

AN AFRICAN DESERT

The Atacama Desert in Chile has been almost rainless for more than 400 years!

Which place on Earth gets the most rain?

A spot on the Hawaiian island of Kauai (kah-oo-AH-ee) gets about 460 inches of rain each year. That's at least 400 inches more than most other places in the United States.

THUNDER AND LIGHTNING

What causes thunderstorms?

We have thunderstorms when big, fluffy-looking clouds, called thunder-heads, tower very high into the sky. They look beautiful when you see them at a distance. When the sun shines on their high-piled puffs, they look white, but as they sweep overhead and shut out the sunlight, they look very dark.

These clouds build up on hot, damp days when the very warm ground heats the moist air above it. The air rises higher and faster than usual. Water droplets gather into very big clouds. Some are several miles high! Inside each cloud, the warm, rising air cools quickly and sinks to a lower part of the cloud. There, the air is warmed again, and it rises. This rising and falling air makes violent winds inside the cloud. Large raindrops form, lightning flashes, and thunder crashes.

After a lightning bolt this size, loud thunder is sure to follow.

What is lightning?

Lightning is a flash of electricity in the air. There is electricity everywhere—in clouds, in the Earth, even in you! Sometimes when you walk across a carpet and touch someone, you feel a tiny spark of electricity jump between the two of you.

In towering thunderclouds, a lot of electricity builds up. As clouds draw near one another, huge flashes of electricity pass between two clouds, or from a cloud to Earth. The electricity heats the air along the path of the flash so much that the air glows. That glow is what we call lightning.

Each second of every day, about 100 bolts of lightning strike some part of the Earth!

What is thunder?

When air is heated, the very tiny particles that make it up begin to move faster. The electrical flash from a thundercloud suddenly heats the air so much that all the particles move around wildly. The air shakes, as huge numbers of them suddenly rush apart. When this sudden huge movement in the air reaches our ears, we hear a thunderclap.

Why do you see the lightning before you hear the thunder?

Light travels fast—186,282 miles in one second! So you see the glow of lightning the instant it flashes, even though it may be miles away. Sound travels much more slowly. It takes the sound of thunder nearly five seconds to travel one mile. So if a lightning flash is one mile away, you see the light right away. Then the sky darkens again, and after about five seconds, you hear the thunder.

ARGH!

Can thunder and lightning hurt you?

Thunder can't hurt you, but lightning can. Thunder is just air shaking very hard. Lightning is electricity. A very small flash of electricity can give you a shock. A lightning flash is huge. It can burn whatever it touches, sometimes very badly.

Lightning usually strikes the highest thing around. This may be a skyscraper in a city, a tall tree in an open field, or a sailboat mast on the water. Metal lightning rods or specially wired television antennas can lead the electricity safely to the ground. They can keep a building safe from lightning damage. A metal car or airplane body can protect people inside it, too. However, if you stand under a big tree, you will not be protected. The tree may be hit by lightning, and so may you. So if you are outside during a thunderstorm, you will be safest lying flat on the ground!

About 40,000 thunderstorms occur each day on Earth!

FREEZING RAIN AND SNOW

Hailstones come in many shapes and sizes.

What is hail?

Hail is made up of small lumps of ice that sometimes fall to Earth during thunderstorms. These icy stones are formed inside the thunderclouds. The tops of tall thunderheads are always very cold. Down near the bottoms of the clouds, the air is much warmer. Inside these clouds, warm air moves swiftly up, and cold air moves swiftly down. Sometimes raindrops are blown up to the freezing-cold part of the cloud before they fall. There they turn to ice. Then they are blown down again and are coated with more raindrops. Before they fall to Earth, the bits of ice may be blown up and down many times. Each time, more raindrops gather on them and then freeze, forming extra layers of ice on the lump. Each lump of ice is called a hailstone.

Hailstones as big as your head have fallen. Some have measured 17½ inches around!

What is sleet?

Sleet is frozen rain. It falls when the air close to the ground is freezing cold. Sleet starts out as rain. As the raindrops fall, they freeze. They form the tiny ice balls known as sleet.

Is snow frozen rain?

No. Raindrops that freeze as they fall form sleet, not snow. Snowflakes are formed right in the clouds. Clouds floating in freezing-cold air are made up of tiny crystals of ice. As the air grows colder, more and more water vapor condenses around the ice. The tiny crystals grow bigger and bigger. The snowflakes you see are simply these crystals after they have grown too large and heavy to float in the air. They fall to Earth as snow.

What do snowflakes look like?

If you look closely at a group of snowflakes, you will see that they are like small, lacy crystals. Snowflakes have many different sizes, shapes, and lovely patterns. However, if you count their sides, you will find that each snowflake has six sides, and each has six points, too.

No two snowflakes are exactly alike!

CHAPTER 12

Planet Earth wouldn't be the same without green fields of clover, giant redwood trees, and colorful flowers. You'll find some plants on your dinner table as vege-tables. Plants also perform a special task that gives us air to breathe! Let's take a look at the amazing plants in our world.

THE EARTH IN BLOOM!

ALL ABOUT PLANTS

What is a plant?

Anything that is alive and isn't an animal is a plant. Unlike animals, most plants stay in one place. They don't walk, swim, or fly. Most plants have green leaves, which contain the chemical compound chlorophyll (KLAWR-uh-fill). Chlorophyll gives leaves their green color. Some plants with chlorophyll don't have green leaves. They have red, purple, or brown leaves instead.

How many kinds of plants are there?

There are more than 360,000 different kinds of plants on the Earth. They come in all sizes. Some are so tiny that you can see them only under a microscope. Others are so large that they tower hundreds of feet above the ground. In fact, the tallest living thing, the giant redwood tree, is a plant.

Plants have many different shapes, too. A blade of grass is long and skinny. Palm trees have large leaves and long trunks. Cabbages are round and leafy. A cactus is narrow with sharp spines. Mushrooms are umbrella-shaped, and lichens (LIKE-inz) spread out like a carpet.

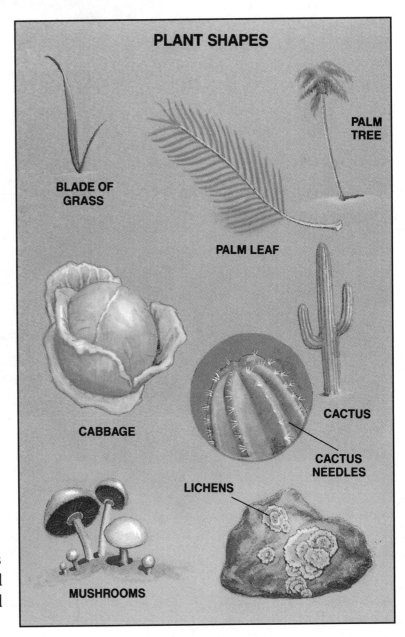

PLANT SHAPES

BLADE OF GRASS

PALM LEAF

PALM TREE

CABBAGE

CACTUS

CACTUS NEEDLES

LICHENS

MUSHROOMS

How can you tell how old a tree is?

Each ring in a tree shows one year's growth.

When a tree is cut down, you can usually see rings in the tree stump. The rings show how many years the tree was growing.

Each spring, a tree grows new wood. This light-colored wood grows around the old, dark wood of the tree trunk. So if you count the number of dark-colored rings, you will know how many years the tree lived.

How long have plants been on the Earth?

Plants have been on the Earth for more than 400 million years. The first plants were tiny water plants, the kind you can see only under a microscope. They were on the Earth about 200 million years before the dinosaurs. In fact, they were here long before any animals.

Some bristlecone pine trees have lived nearly 5,000 years!

What would happen if all the plants on the Earth died?

If all the plants on the Earth died, so would all the animals, including people. We need plants in order to live. When plants make food, they give off oxygen (OCK-suh-jin), a gas that animals must breathe in order to stay alive.

Animals also depend on plants for their food. All animals eat either plants or plant-eating animals. Without plants, there would be almost no food on the Earth! All of the animals on Earth would die.

SEEDS

What's inside a seed?

The inside of every seed has a soft part called an embryo (EM-bree-oh). A new plant starts from the embryo and the soft food stored around it.

To make seeds, most flowers need pollen from another flower. When pollen from one flower gets on another, the plant is pollinated (POLL-in-ate-ed). Bees and wind help pollinate flowers.

SEED

SHELL

EMBRYO

How does a seed become a new plant?

The embryo forms while the seed is still on the plant. Once it is formed, it stops growing for a while. It will grow—germinate (GER-min-ate)—as soon as it is in the right soil with the right temperature and the right amount of water. Then the embryo will sprout roots and stems. It will grow leaves and start making its own food. The embryo will become a whole plant and make seeds of its own.

The feathery seeds of this flower are carried by the wind.

Do all new plants come from seeds?

Plants that have flowers come from seeds. Other plants start in other ways. Some plants send out long horizontal stems above the ground, called runners, to start new plants. Strawberries start plants this way. The leaf of some plants, such as the African violet, can be put into the ground, and new plants will grow from it. Other plants grow plantlets. These are whole plants that are smaller than the parent, but otherwise just like it. The plantlet stays attached to the parent until it grows to nearly full size. Then it splits off from the parent plant and lives on its own. Other plants grow tiny specks, called spores, instead of seeds. Each spore can produce a new plant. Look under the umbrella of a mushroom or on the underside of a fern leaf to see spores.

How are seeds spread so that plants grow in many different places?

The wind spreads seeds that are tiny or fluffy and can easily float in the air. It also spreads seeds that have "wings," such as maple seeds.

Water sometimes spreads these winged seeds, too. Any seeds that are able to float can be spread by water. Such seeds may travel long distances before they reach land again.

Animals also spread seeds. Some seeds have sharp hooks that get stuck to an animal's fur and fall off later. Burrs, or "stickers," are seeds of this kind. Some birds and other animals eat the fruits of trees. They may carry off the fruits and then drop the seeds far away.

POOF!

THE RESEMBLANCE IS UNCANNY!

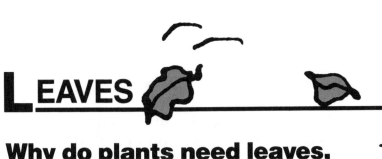

LEAVES

Why do plants need leaves, roots, flowers, and stems?

Most plants make their own food. They use their leaves to make it.

Roots are needed to hold a plant firmly in the ground. The roots also take water and minerals out of the soil. The plant needs these things to live. Sometimes roots store some of the food that the leaves make.

Flowers are the parts of the plant where seeds can form. The seeds will someday be new plants.

Stems hold up the leaves and flowers to sunlight. Stems have tubes in them that carry liquids, called sap, up and down the plant. Some of the tubes bring water mixed with minerals from the roots to the leaves. Other tubes carry liquid food away from the leaves to the rest of the plant.

The largest flowering plant growing on Earth today is a Chinese wisteria (wiss-STEER-ee-uh). It has branches 500 feet long, and it weighs as much as 50 elephants!

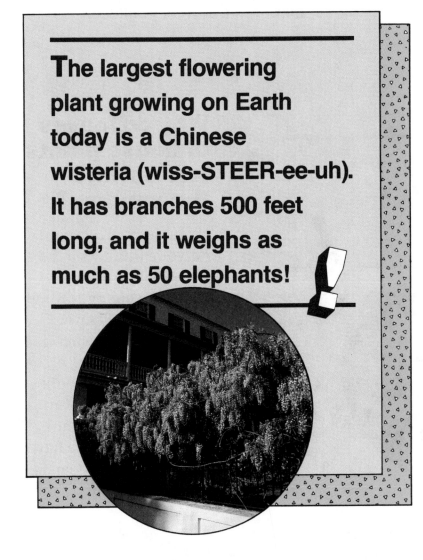

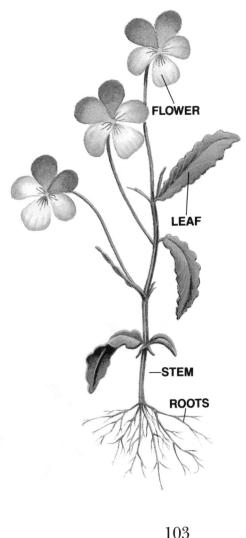

FLOWER

LEAF

—STEM

ROOTS

How do leaves make food?

The leaves of a plant are like little food factories. Inside them is the chemical chlorophyll that the leaves need to make food. The food factory needs sun to start working. When the Sun shines on the chlorophyll, each leaf factory goes to work.

The leaf factory uses two things to make food. It uses water that has come up from the soil through the roots and stems. It also uses a gas called carbon dioxide (die-OCK-side) that has come from the air through tiny openings in the leaf. From the water and carbon dioxide it makes sugar, which is the plant's food. At the same time, the factory makes a gas called oxygen. The plant sends this oxygen into the air.

Without any sunlight (or an electric plant light), plants cannot make food, and they will die.

SUN
WATER
AIR
SOIL

A "food factory"

A pine needle is really a leaf! And a pinecone is a kind of flower.

Why do leaves of house plants turn toward the window?

If you let a plant stand on your windowsill, its leaves will turn toward the light coming through the window. Plants need the light to make food. This turning of plants toward the light is called phototropism (foe-toe-TRO-piz-em).

Outdoors, plants have light all around them, so their leaves don't turn.

Why do leaves change color in the fall?

Leaves have many colors in them—green, red, orange, and yellow—but during the spring and summer, there is much more green than any other color. The green comes from the chlorophyll. The leaves have so much chlorophyll that it hides the other colors and you can't see them. In the fall, however, before cold weather sets in, many leaves stop making food. When they stop making food, the chlorophyll breaks down. As it breaks down, the colors that were hidden start to appear, and you can see them in the leaves.

Why do leaves drop off the trees in the fall?

During warm weather, the leaves of a tree are always giving off tiny drops of water. At the same time, the tree's roots are taking in more water so that the tree does not dry out. During cold weather, however, the ground freezes. The roots cannot get much water. If the leaves kept giving off water, the tree would dry up and die.

In the fall, a layer of cork grows at the bottom of each leaf stem, blocking water from flowing into the leaf. The leaf dries up. It is easily shaken off the tree by the wind, and it falls to the ground.

• The hottest temperature ever recorded was in the country of Libya in North Africa. There, in one place in 1922, the temperature reached more than 136 degrees Fahrenheit! If you look at an air thermometer, you will see that the numbers on it don't even go that high!

• The place with the coldest temperature on record is near the South Pole. At a weather station called Vostok, 400 miles from the Pole, the temperature has gotten colder than 126 degrees below zero Fahrenheit. You'd need warm clothes in weather that cold!

• Some plants eat animals! These plants can make their own food, but they need additional minerals that they cannot get from the soil. They get this extra food from the insects, small birds, or mice that they eat! Three of the animal-eating plants are the pitcher plant, the sundew, and the Venus's-flytrap. The pitcher plant has leaves shaped like pitchers or vases. The bottom of each pitcher contains water. If an insect, bird, or mouse falls inside, it drowns. The sundew has leaves covered with many hairs. At the tip of each hair is a sticky liquid that shines like dew in the sunlight. When an insect lands on a leaf, it gets caught in the sticky drops. The hairs bend over the insect and hold it down as the plant digests it. The Venus's-flytrap has leaves that fold in half and close like a trap. Each leaf has little hairs on it. When an insect lands on the hairs, the two halves of the leaf close, trapping the insect. When the plant has finished eating, the leaf opens up again, to wait for another victim.

I GAVE MY REPORT IN SCHOOL TODAY...

AT THE END I SAID, "THIS REPORT WAS WRITTEN ON RECYCLED PAPER..NO TREES WERE DESTROYED TO MAKE THIS REPORT"

DID THE TEACHER APPRECIATE IT?

NO, BUT THE TREES DID!

● Every day we use things that come from plants. Things made of wood—houses, fences, furniture, and paper—come from the trunks of trees.

Rubber comes from the sap of the rubber tree. Tires, shoe heels, rubber balls, diving suits, and many toys are made of rubber.

Cotton cloth is made from the cotton plant, and linen cloth is made from the flax plant. Clothes, curtains, and sheets are some of the things made from cotton and linen.

Medicines, too, come from plants. Quinine, used to treat malaria, comes from the bark of the cinchona (sin-KOE-nuh) tree. Digitalis (dij-ih-TAL-iss), used to treat weak hearts, is made from the dried leaves of the foxglove plant.

● Old Faithful is a geyser (GUY-zur) in Yellowstone National Park, Wyoming. A geyser is a special kind of hot spring. Its water gets so hot underground that it boils and explodes into steam. The geyser shoots the hot water and steam into the air from an opening in the ground. The water shoots up like a fountain for a while, and then dies down.

Some geysers spurt only once every few years. Old Faithful got its name by shooting

water faithfully about once every 30 to 80 minutes for more than 100 years. It shoots the water more than 130 feet high!

● Rainbows are made when sunlight shines through moisture in the sky. The tiny drops of water break the light into beautiful colors.

EVEN I LIKE RAINBOWS!

Look up into the night sky. The Moon glows brightly, and, as far as your eyes can see, the stars sparkle like tiny diamonds. What lies beyond the Earth, the Moon, and the stars, which seem to go on forever? Let's take a trip through our incredible universe and find out!

YOUR AMAZING UNIVERSE

CHAPTER 13

LET'S MEET THE UNIVERSE—GALAXIES AND OUR SOLAR SYSTEM

What is the universe?

The word *universe* means everything there is—the Moon, the Sun, the Earth, the other planets, the stars, and anything else you can think of. All of space and everything in space is part of the universe. It extends much, much farther than you could see with the most powerful of all telescopes. Most scientists believe that there is an end to the universe, but no one knows where the end is.

How did the universe form?

Most scientists believe the universe began with a giant explosion—a big bang. This probably happened between 10 and 20 billion years ago. Before the explosion, all the material or "matter" in the universe was packed together tightly. The explosion blew it apart, sending hot gases and matter flying in every direction! After hundreds of millions of years, galaxies were formed from the swirling gases of the explosion. Later, stars and planets formed from the gases remaining in each galaxy.

THERE ARE SO MANY STARS AND PLANETS...IT'S HARD TO KEEP TRACK OF THEM!

Outer space is filled with faint radio waves. Some scientists believe these are the dying radio echoes of the Big Bang!

What is a galaxy?

A galaxy is a huge cluster of stars held close together by gravity. "Close together" for stars means they're actually billions of miles apart! Through a telescope, galaxies look like islands. Each one contains billions of stars. Scientists don't know how many galaxies there are in the universe, but they believe there may be 100 billion!

What is a star made of?

When you look up at the sky on a clear night, you see many, many twinkling stars. These points of light are really huge balls of bright, hot, glowing gases. They pour out light, just the way the Sun does. In fact, the Sun *is* a star. The other stars look much smaller than the Sun because they are much farther away from the Earth.

If you counted one star per second, it would take you more than 12,000 years to count the 400 billion stars in a normal galaxy!

What galaxy is Earth in?

Our own star—the Sun—and the Earth and other planets are all part of the Milky Way galaxy. From one part of space, far beyond our galaxy, the whole galaxy would appear as one big band of light with a bulge in the middle. From another part of space beyond our galaxy, the Milky Way would appear as a glowing spiral-shaped island. Our own Sun would appear as a medium-sized star on one of the spiral's starry arms.

If you looked at the night sky from a place far from city lights, you might see the Milky Way as a glowing band of light stretching across the sky. This band is made up of billions of stars. You cannot see the separate stars in the band without using a telescope because the stars are so far away from us.

The glowing band is actually only part of the galaxy that we call the Milky Way. This galaxy includes all the separate stars we see in the night sky. These stars are closer to the Earth than the band is, so we don't see them all blurred together.

THE MILKY WAY

What is a solar system?

A solar system is a family of planets and other objects that orbit, or travel around, a star. That star is a Sun. The Sun's family consists of planets, asteroids, comets, and meteors. Many scientists think that there could be planets orbiting many stars. This would mean that there are many solar systems!

What is our solar system?

The Sun and all the objects that orbit it—including the Earth—form our solar system. The Sun is at the center of our solar system. The Sun's gravity is a pulling force much stronger than the gravity of Earth. The Sun's gravity, along with the movement of each planet, keeps the planets in their paths around the Sun. Without the Sun's gravity, each planet would fly off into space. Without its own path, each planet would fall into the Sun!

CHAPTER 14

From space it looks like a big blue marble. Scientists think it's the only planet in the solar system that has living beings. It's also the only planet with flowing water on its surface. Have you guessed which planet we're talking about? It's your very own home—Earth!

NO PLACE LIKE HOME

HOME SWEET HOME

EARTH FACTS

When was the Earth formed?

Many scientists believe that the Earth was probably formed about five billion years ago. At first the Earth's air was poisonous, and there was no life. Over billions of years, the Earth changed. Now the Earth provides the energy, warmth, water, and air we need to keep us alive.

How big is the Earth?

If you could dig a tunnel through the center of the Earth from one side to the other, your tunnel would be almost 8,000 miles long. That distance is greater than 140,000 football fields placed end to end. If you walked around the Earth, you'd have to walk almost 25,000 miles—some 440,000 football fields!

Even though the Earth seems like a very big place, the Sun is much bigger. The Sun is 108 times wider than the Earth. It's so much bigger than the Earth that you could fit more than one million planets the size of the Earth inside the Sun!

In the sixth century B.C., a man named Pythagoras (pi-THAG-or-us) claimed that the Earth was shaped like a ball. Most people didn't believe him. They thought the Earth was flat!

How much does Earth weigh?

Our planet weighs about 6,600 million trillion tons.

What star is closest to Earth?

The Sun is our closest star. Other stars look much smaller than the Sun because they are much farther away from the Earth. Actually, many other stars in our universe are bigger than the Sun.

The Sun is actually a star.

How far is the Earth from the Sun?

The Sun is 93 million miles away from us. That may sound very far away, but it takes only eight minutes for the Sun's light to reach us. The Sun is close enough to give the Earth light and heat.

If the Sun were the size of a large orange, the Earth would be the size of a tiny seed about 33 feet away!

WHEN WILL HE REALIZE HE'LL NEVER KICK THAT BALL OFF THE EARTH!

boot! boot! boot! boot! boot! boot!

Why can't a football fall off the Earth?

A football, or any other object, cannot fall off the Earth because it is always pulled toward the Earth by gravity. This invisible force draws all things on the Earth toward its center.

115

THE EARTH RACING THROUGH SPACE

How long does it take the Earth to orbit the Sun?

The Earth takes a little more than 365 days to orbit the Sun. That's how long one year lasts on the Earth.

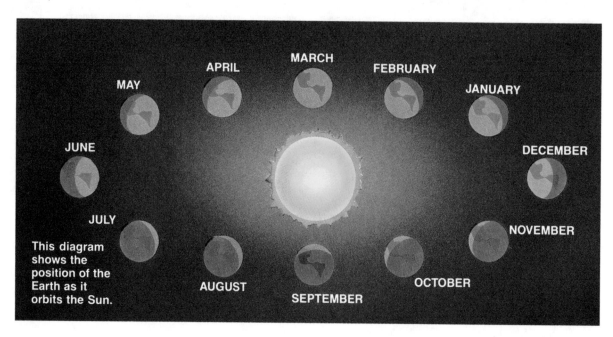

MARCH APRIL MAY JUNE JULY AUGUST SEPTEMBER OCTOBER NOVEMBER DECEMBER JANUARY FEBRUARY

This diagram shows the position of the Earth as it orbits the Sun.

How fast does the Earth travel around the Sun?

Scientists have figured out that the Earth is racing through space at about 67,000 miles an hour—thousands of times faster than the fastest racing car. During the time it took you to read this answer, the Earth probably moved through space more than 300 miles!

Why don't you feel the Earth moving?

You can't feel the Earth moving through space because it moves so smoothly. When you ride in a car, you know you're moving, even if you close your eyes. That's because the ride is bumpy. When you are on a jet plane and you close your eyes, most of the time you cannot tell the plane is moving. That's because the ride is smooth. The movement of the Earth through space is even smoother, so you cannot feel it at all.

The Earth is moving with the Sun and the rest of the solar system through space. Because of this motion, even though we are carried around the Sun year after year, the Earth never returns to the same place in space twice!

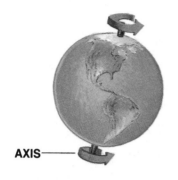

AXIS

What makes the Sun rise?

The Sun doesn't rise; the Earth turns. The Earth is always turning on its axis, an imaginary line that goes through the North and South poles. This motion of the Earth on its axis is called rotation (row-TAY-shun).

What happens when the Earth rotates?

If you have a globe and a flashlight, you can do an experiment to see why the Sun seems to rise. Place a lamp or flashlight so that it shines on the globe. Pretend that the light is sunlight. You can see that the light is hitting only one part of the globe. Now turn the globe slowly. As the globe turns, a different part of the globe is lighted. In the same way, as the Earth turns, a different part of the Earth gets sunlight. When the side of the Earth you live on isn't facing the Sun, you have night. When the Earth turns farther around, the part you live on comes into the sunlight. Then the Sun seems to rise in the sky, and you have daylight. Because the Earth rotates, the stars also seem to rise and set like the Sun. For the same reason, you also see the Moon rise and set.

If the Earth didn't move, half of the world would always be in sunlight, and the other half would always be dark. Aren't you glad that the Earth rotates?

The ancient Egyptians believed that the Sun hatched each day from the egg of a heavenly goose!

If you live in New England, you have four seasons with varying weather.

MARCH

JUNE

DECEMBER

SEPTEMBER

Why do we have seasons?

As you've learned, it takes a year for the Earth to make one trip around the Sun. The Earth's axis doesn't point straight up and down, so the Earth tilts to one side as it travels around the Sun. This tilt gives us our four seasons.

In summer, when the part of the Earth you live on tilts toward the Sun, you get the most hours of sunlight and heat. In the fall, your part of the Earth begins to tilt away from the Sun, and you get less sunlight and heat. In winter, when your part of the Earth tilts still farther away from the Sun, you get even less sunlight and heat. In the spring, your part of the Earth tilts closer to the Sun again, and you get more hours of sunlight and heat.

CHAPTER 15

Ready to go next door for a visit? Next door in space, that is! The Moon is Earth's closest neighbor. You can see it glowing in the sky most nights, and some Earthlings have even traveled there already. Would you like to take a journey to the Moon? Well, come along!

THE MOON UP CLOSE

MOON FACTS

Where did the Moon come from?

According to many scientists, the Moon could have been formed in several ways. One possibility is that both the Earth and Moon may have formed about five billion years ago, with the larger Earth "capturing" the smaller Moon in its gravity. Another possibility is that the Moon formed from some kind of collision of two larger planets when the solar system first began five billion years ago. Scientists don't know which idea is right, but many believe that the age of the Earth and Moon are the same—about five billion years.

How big is the Moon?

The Moon might look large when it's full, but the Earth is almost four times larger. Even so, the Moon is almost as wide as the United States. A tunnel through the Moon would be 2,160 miles long!

I GUESS IT'S A LITTLE TOO FAR TO WALK THERE.

How far from the Earth is the Moon?

The Moon is about 239,000 miles away from the Earth. That's almost 80 times the distance between New York and California!

Why does the Moon shine?

The Moon does not shine with its own light. It has no light to give out. The Moon reflects, or sends back, light rays that come to it from the Sun. Those light rays reach the Earth—and your eyes.

Just as the Sun shines on part of the Earth at all times, the Sun shines on part of the Moon at all times. The Moon is always reflecting some sunlight, but you cannot always see it. During the day, the Sun shines on the part of the Earth where you live. The Sun's light is brighter than the Moon's light, so the sunlight usually hides the Moon from your sight. At night, no sunlight hides the Moon, so you can see it "shining" unless it's hidden by clouds.

The Sun's rays bounce off not only the Moon, but also the Earth. If you were out in space, you would see the Earth shining more brightly than the Moon!

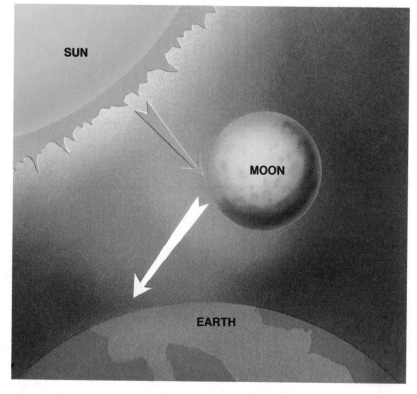

Light rays from the Sun bounce off the Moon, which enables us to see the Moon from Earth.

SUN

MOON

EARTH

What does the Moon look like close up?

The Moon is very rough and rocky. It has tall mountains, deep cracks, and steep cliffs. All over the Moon are thousands of deep holes shaped like saucers. These holes are called craters. Many of them were formed when rocks flying through space crashed into the Moon. Most of these flying rocks were moving so fast that they shattered when they hit the Moon. Bits of them were scattered all over, so you cannot find the rocks, but you can see the holes they made. Some craters are less than a foot wide. Others are nearly 150 miles wide.

I THINK YOU STEPPED IN A CRATER, SIR.

The crater Copernicus is one of the easiest craters on the Moon for us to see. The bottom of the crater is nearly 50 miles across. The mountains at the rim of the crater are nearly 12,000 feet high, a climb of more than 2 miles for a future astronaut!

What are the dark areas on the Moon's surface?

The dark areas we have discovered on the surface of the Moon are called *maria*, which means seas. But these seas aren't like the seas on Earth. Billions of years ago, large asteroids hit the surface of the Moon. This created huge basins or holes. Many years later, these basins were filled with melted rock. When this rock cooled on the Moon's surface, it formed these dark spots. Some spots are very big. The largest is about 700 miles across.

A closeup view of the Moon.

Small moonquakes rock the Moon about 3,000 times every year!

THERE IT GOES AGAIN!

Can anything live on the Moon?

Because the Moon has no air or water, people, plants, and animals cannot live there. American astronauts have visited the Moon by bringing supplies with them. However, scientists have found that, with air and water, plants can grow in Moon soil that the astronauts brought back to Earth.

THE MOON IN MOTION

Why do we see only one side of the Moon?

Just as the Earth moves in two different ways, the Moon also moves in two different ways. It turns on its axis, and it travels in its orbit around the Earth. The Moon takes 27 days, 7 hours, and 43 minutes to turn around once on its axis—about the same amount of time it takes the Moon to travel once around the Earth. This means that the Moon always keeps the same side facing the Earth. From the Earth you never see the other side of the Moon.

Does the Moon really control the ocean's tides?

Yes, it does. The Moon has its own gravity, just as the Earth and all other planets do. The Moon's pull on the Earth isn't strong enough for us to notice on land, although there are instruments that can measure it. We do see its effect on the seas, however. As the Moon travels around the Earth, its gravity pulls up the seas. When that happens, we say it is high tide. As the Moon passes away, the seas flow back to low tide.

125

PHASES OF THE MOON

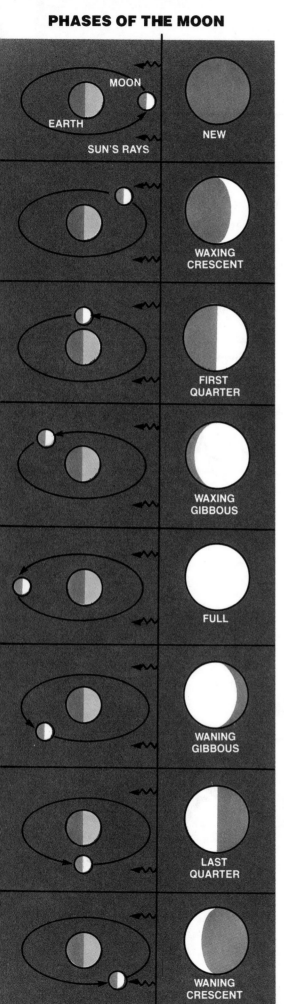

MOON

EARTH

SUN'S RAYS

NEW

WAXING CRESCENT

FIRST QUARTER

WAXING GIBBOUS

FULL

WANING GIBBOUS

LAST QUARTER

WANING CRESCENT

Why doesn't the Moon always look round?

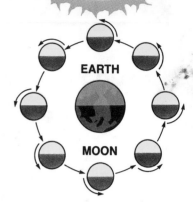

SUN

EARTH

MOON

As we've learned, the Moon has no light of its own. Light comes to it from the Sun, just as light comes to the Earth from the Sun. A part of the Moon is always turned toward the Sun, and a part of it is always turned away from the Sun. One part is as dark as night. The other part is as bright as day. We see the Moon only when some of the lighted part is turned toward the Earth.

As the Moon travels around the Earth, it always keeps the same side facing the Earth. We can't always see all of that side, however, because different amounts of it are lighted by the Sun during different days of the month. Sometimes, then, we see just a sliver. Sometimes we see a half Moon, and sometimes we see a full Moon.

The different shapes of the Moon are called phases. The Moon goes through all its phases every 29 to 30 days.

No one had seen the far side of the Moon until 1959, when a Soviet spacecraft took the first photos of it!

AN ECLIPSE OF THE MOON

What causes an eclipse of the Moon?

When the Sun shines on them, the Earth and Moon cast shadows into space. An eclipse of the Moon happens when the Moon moves behind the Earth and into the Earth's shadow. Because the Moon is in this shadow, most of the Sun's light cannot hit the Moon, and you can barely see it. What you do see of the Moon looks reddish. When the Moon comes out from the Earth's shadow, it shines again with full light from the Sun. The eclipse is over.

Can the Moon's shadow cause an eclipse of the Sun?

Yes, it can. Even though the Moon is much smaller than the Sun, it is so close to us that when the Moon moves directly in front of the Sun, it blocks the Sun's light, and casts a shadow on part of the Earth. If you are in one of those shadowy places, you see an eclipse—the round disk of the Moon passing across the face of the Sun.

Because looking straight at the Sun can harm your eyes, you should never do it—even during an eclipse. Scientists who study eclipses have special equipment which allows them to view an eclipse of the Sun safely. Eclipses of the Moon are not dangerous to look at.

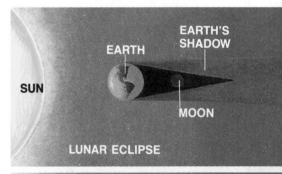

LUNAR ECLIPSE

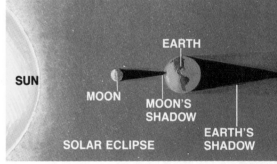

SOLAR ECLIPSE

THAT'S TOTALLY COOL!

What's the difference between a total eclipse and a partial eclipse?

Total eclipse means that the whole Sun or the whole Moon is blocked from view. Partial eclipse means that only a part of the Moon or the Sun is blocked out. Partial eclipses happen when the Earth, Moon, and Sun do not line up exactly.

127

Our Sun is only one of billions of stars in our galaxy, but it's very important to us. After all, without the Sun's rays, we wouldn't have any light or heat! What would you see if you could travel close to the Sun? Let's discover the Sun's secrets.

OUR MIGHTY SUN

SUN FACTS

What is the Sun made of?

Hydrogen and helium are the two main gases that make up the Sun. Hydrogen is the Sun's fuel. Every second, millions of tons of hydrogen in the Sun's center, or core, change into helium. This change, called nuclear fusion, releases lots of energy.

HOW HOT IS THE SUN? TOO HOT!

GOOD GRIEF!

How hot is the Sun?

The temperature of the outer part of the Sun is about 10,000 degrees Fahrenheit. Any metal known on Earth would melt at such a high temperature. Most other things on Earth would burn up. The inside of the Sun is even hotter than the outside. Scientists think that the temperature at the Sun's center is about 27 million degrees Fahrenheit.

Where does the Sun's energy go?

After many years, energy released in the Sun's core rises to its surface and travels into space. Part of this energy becomes our sunshine, which takes a little more than eight minutes to reach the Earth!

Never look directly at the Sun. The strong light can easily blind you!

What is solar wind?

The Sun gives off a stream of gases flowing out in all directions. This is called solar wind. This wind travels all the way through our solar system. It even blows beyond Pluto, the planet that is farthest from the Sun.

The Earth is usually protected from solar wind by two magnetic belts. When there's lots of activity on the Sun's surface, however, some particles do get through to reach the Earth. When these particles collide with particles in the atmosphere near the North and South poles of the Earth, a glowing effect called an aurora (ah-ROAR-ah) occurs. Auroras create a beautiful colored light show in the Earth's sky. In the Northern Hemisphere, this show of lights is called the aurora borealis (ah-ROAR-ah bore-ee-AL-is).

Does the Sun rotate in space?

The Sun rotates on its own axis, but it doesn't do so in the same way that our Earth does. Gases in the middle of the Sun rotate faster than those at the top and bottom do.

The Sun takes more than 25 days to rotate once at its middle, while gases at the top and bottom rotate once in nearly 29 days! Our Earth is solid, so all of it rotates every 24 hours.

ON THE SURFACE OF THE SUN

What is the surface of the Sun like?

The Sun's surface swirls with hot gases. Sometimes, long streams of gas shoot out, then loop back to the Sun's surface. These arch-shaped fountains of burning gas are called prominences (PROM-ih-nen-sez).

The greatest prominence ever recorded shot 250,000 miles from the surface of the Sun! That's more than the distance between the Moon and the Earth!

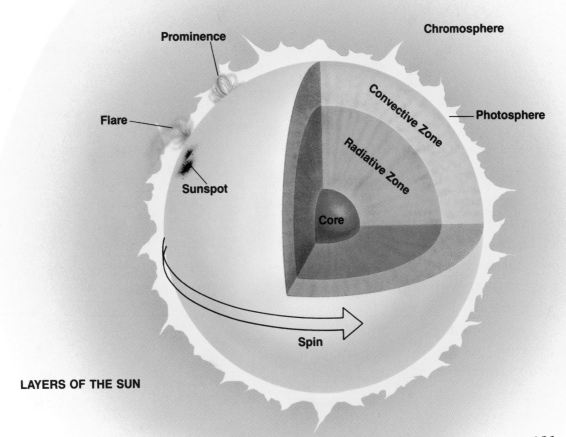

LAYERS OF THE SUN

Prominence

Chromosphere

Flare

Convective Zone

Radiative Zone

Photosphere

Sunspot

Core

Spin

What are sunspots?

Sunspots are dark patches on the surface of the Sun. These spots are cooler than the rest of the Sun's surface, so they shine less brightly. They may last only a few hours or as long as a few weeks.

Eight Earths can fit into the area of one of the larger sunspots!

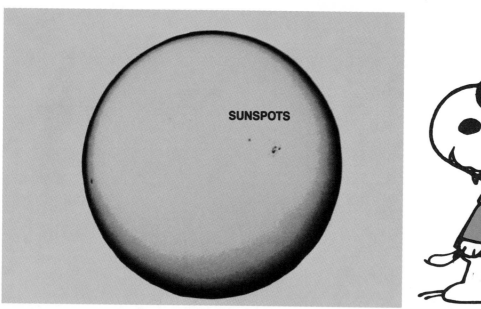

SUNSPOTS

How do scientists study the Sun's surface?

Since looking directly at the Sun can damage your eyes, scientists study the Sun by using special instruments that reflect its light. The McMath Telescope in Arizona is one of these instruments. It is the world's largest solar telescope.

Each day, a large mirror at the top of a tower reflects sunlight down a long tunnel to an underground room. There, another mirror reflects the Sun's image to a special observing room. In this room, scientific instruments are kept at a cool, constant temperature because the intense heat of the Sun's rays could damage them. Even small changes in temperature would upset the instruments used to study the Sun.

By studying the Sun, scientists hope to find out what makes its energy change from day to day, and how the Sun's energy affects life on Earth.

CHAPTER 17

Ready to explore? The planets in space have so many secrets to reveal. So zip up your space suit and follow the *Peanuts* gang on an exciting voyage through our solar system. We'll start at the planet closest to the Sun. First stop: Mercury!

THE FAMILY OF THE SUN

SPACE TRAVEL AGENCY

THE AGENT IS IN

SOLAR SYSTEM FACTS

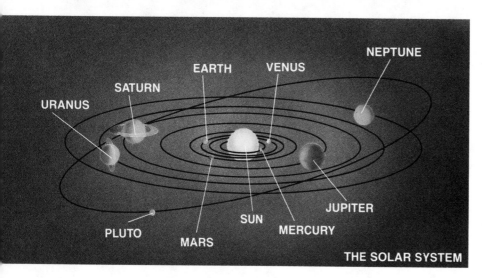

THE SOLAR SYSTEM

What are the names of the planets in the solar system?

The planet closest to the Sun is called Mercury. Then come Venus, Earth, Mars, Jupiter, Saturn, Uranus, Neptune and Pluto.

THAT'S GRAVITY FOR YOU!

Does the solar system move?

Yes. The Sun and all its planets are traveling around the center of our galaxy. The whole solar system is moving at the speed of 175 miles a second around the center of the Milky Way galaxy!

Is the Earth the only planet with gravity?

No. Each planet has gravity. That means that Mars pulls things toward its center. Pluto pulls things toward its center. So do Saturn, Jupiter, and all the others. In fact, everything in the universe has gravity—even a pencil and a grain of sand. Of course, the bigger the object is, the stronger its pull. A tiny satellite doesn't have much gravity, so a spaceship at equal distance between a planet and a satellite would be pulled toward the planet. Stars have the greatest gravity because they are bigger than any other objects in the universe. The Sun's strong pull keeps the planets in orbit around it.

134

Can we see any of the nine planets without a telescope?

THE MOON

VENUS

Sometimes planets such as Venus appear as stars in the night sky.

Yes, we can see Saturn, Mercury, Venus, Mars, and Jupiter. Mercury is hard to see because it is often close to the Sun and hidden by its glare. You can usually tell when you're looking at a planet in the night sky because it shines with a bright, steady light. The planets, except for Mercury, don't twinkle the way stars do.

Some scientists have been able to see Uranus without a telescope because they know exactly where to look in the sky. They also make their observations far from city lights, where the sky is clear and dark!

The first star you see in the night sky may not be a star at all. It could be a planet—either Mercury, Venus, Mars, Jupiter, or Saturn!

Which of the planets, besides Earth, have moons?

Mars has 2 moons called Phobos and Deimos. Jupiter has 16 moons. Scientists have seen 17 moons around Saturn, 15 around Uranus, and 8 around Neptune. The farthest planet, Pluto, has 1 moon. Each moon travels in an orbit around its planet.

STARLIGHT, STAR BRIGHT, FIRST STAR I SEE TONIGHT. WISH I MAY. WISH I MIGHT. HAVE THE WISH I WISH TONIGHT.

DON'T TELL HIM IT'S A PLANET!

MERCURY, VENUS, AND MARS

What are the inner planets?

Mercury, Venus, and Mars, along with the Earth, are sometimes called the inner planets because they are the nearest to the Sun. These four planets also have something else in common. All are solid, with rocky surfaces.

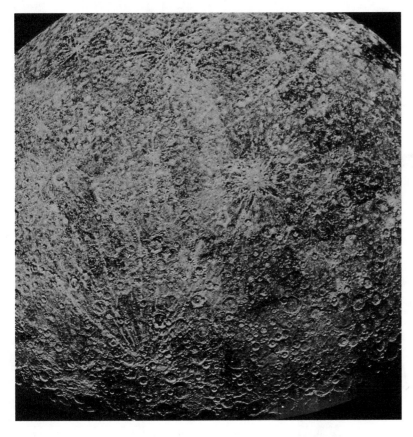

Which planet orbits the Sun the fastest?

Mercury. It travels at about 108,000 miles an hour, and makes one complete orbit of the Sun every three months.

This photo, showing a close view of Mercury, was taken by the space probe Mariner 10.

What is the surface of Mercury like?

Mercury is covered by dust. Craters scar its surface. Some of Mercury's craters are filled with lava. The lava may have come from volcanoes or from rocks that melted when they crashed to the planet's surface.

Because it has hardly any atmosphere, Mercury gets very hot—and very cold. In the daytime, Mercury's temperature can reach 800 degrees Fahrenheit! This is seven times hotter than the hottest desert on Earth. At night, the temperature drops to 300 degrees below zero Fahrenheit.

Mercury goes around the Sun about four times in every Earth year. A person 10 Earth-years old would have gone around the Sun more than 40 times if he or she lived on Mercury!

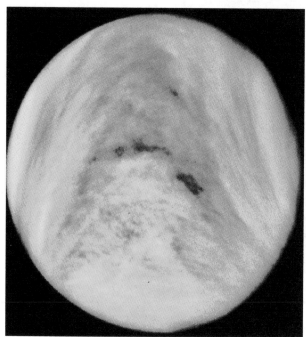

The surface of Venus is a scorching 900 degrees!

Which planet is closest to the Earth?

Venus is the planet closest to the Earth. It is also the second planet from the Sun. It takes 225 days to orbit the Sun. Venus is about the same size as Earth, but the atmosphere on Venus is much heavier than our own. On the surface of Venus, the pressure is 90 times that on Earth. That's equal to the pressure a diver would experience 264 feet under the ocean.

What is the surface of Venus like?

The surface of Venus cannot be seen because it is covered by pale yellow clouds. These clouds let in sunlight, but they do not let the heat out. Because the heat is trapped, Venus gets as hot as 900 degrees Fahrenheit.

138

One of the highest mountains in the solar system is on Venus. Called Maxwell Montes, it is more than a mile higher than Mount Everest!

MY FAVORITE COLOR IS RED!

Has anyone ever visited Venus?

Although people have not traveled to Venus, the United States and the Soviet Union have sent nearly two dozen spacecraft—called probes—to Venus. The first space probe to land on Venus in 1966 was quickly crushed by the planet's heavy atmosphere! Other space probes have sent back images of the dry, rocky planet. The first color television pictures were sent back in 1982. The pictures are sent by television because the probes themselves cannot return to Earth.

What is the "red planet"?

Mars has been called the red planet because it shines like a bright red star. It takes Mars 687 days to orbit the Sun. Scientists think that Mars is cold, dry, and lifeless. Temperatures on the planet range from 80 degrees Fahrenheit to 250 degrees below zero Fahrenheit.

139

Could humans breathe the air on Mars?

You could not breathe the air on Mars. There is no oxygen in it, and it is much thinner than the air on Earth. Since the air on Mars is so thin, it has very little pressure. On Mars, your blood would bubble the same way that a bottle of soda bubbles when the cap is opened.

MARS ROVER

Mars has the largest canyon in the solar system. It is many times longer than the Grand Canyon, and would stretch all the way across the United States!

What does the surface of Mars look like?

If you landed on Mars, you would see a rolling land covered by small rocks. Unmanned spacecraft have analyzed Martian soil—a rusty red dust. These spacecraft have also sent scientists photographs of volcanoes and riverlike canals, but there is no water in these canals.

What's the weather like on Mars?

Mars has four seasons—just as Earth does—but Martian seasons last twice as long because a year on Mars is twice as long as a year on Earth. No rain falls on Mars, but wild dust storms swirl across the planet each summer. White icecaps spread over Mars's north and south poles in the winter. Photographs taken during that season show light patches of frost on one rocky plain.

JUPITER, SATURN, URANUS, NEPTUNE, AND PLUTO

What are the outer planets?

Jupiter, Saturn, Uranus, and Neptune are vast balls of gas circling in the solar system's outer reaches. These four planets are sometimes called the gas giants. They have small rocky centers surrounded by liquid and have thick clouds covering their surfaces. Beyond these four planets lies tiny, frozen Pluto.

Which is the largest planet?

Jupiter, the fifth planet from the Sun. All the other planets could easily fit inside it. Jupiter is larger than 1,300 Earths put together.

JUPITER'S RED SPOT

What is Jupiter's great red spot?

Scientists think this giant spot is a storm that moves on Jupiter's surface. The spot is 9,000 miles wide but in the past has been as large as 30,000 miles wide—much bigger than planet Earth. With a telescope, you can see the spot and follow it around Jupiter. People have been watching the great red spot for more than 300 years!

Jupiter's moon Io (EYE-oh) is the most explosive object in the solar system. Its volcanoes throw up enough material every 3,000 years to cover its own surface!

How long is a year on Jupiter?

One year on Jupiter is equal to almost 12 years on Earth. That's because Jupiter takes nearly 12 Earth years to orbit the Sun. Jupiter spins on its axis very quickly, however. It takes fewer than ten hours for this giant planet to make one turn!

SATURN'S RINGS

What is the second-largest planet in the solar system?

Saturn is the second-biggest planet. It takes almost 30 years to orbit the Sun. Saturn is known for the belt of colorful rings that move around its center.

What are Saturn's rings made of?

Saturn's rings, bands of small particles orbiting the planet, are made of countless pieces of ice, dust and ice-covered rock. These rings have a beautiful golden color when seen through a telescope.

The particles in Saturn's rings move at different speeds as they orbit the planet. The particles in the rings closer to Saturn move faster than the particles in the outer rings. The rings stretch over 40,000 miles, but they are only a few miles thick.

The planet Saturn is large but not very dense. If there were an enormous ocean in space, Saturn would float in it!

THE SEVENTH PLANET, MA'AM, IS DOC...NO, SNEEZY...NO, GRUMPY...NO...

What is the seventh planet from the Sun?

Uranus is the seventh planet from the Sun. It takes 84 years to orbit the Sun. Uranus is covered by methane gas, which gives it a bluish-green color. With temperatures probably reaching 300 degrees below zero Fahrenheit, Uranus is an icy world, far too cold for any living thing. Although it is the third-largest planet, Uranus appears very small, even in a telescope. It is more than 19 times farther from the Sun than the Earth is.

Uranus has a set of narrow rings made of boulder-sized chunks of the darkest material known in the solar system! These rings are so dark that scientists did not discover them until 1977!

Does Uranus have a twin?

Not really. When Neptune was discovered in 1846, scientists could tell that it was similar to Uranus. Both planets are very cold, both have rings, and both look green because of the methane gas in their atmospheres. The planets are similar in size, too. Each is about four times the size of Earth, but Uranus is a little bigger than Neptune. In spite of the similarities, however, the two planets are different enough so that scientists know they are not twins.

What is the weather like on Neptune?

Neptune is covered with layers of cold swirling clouds, so you would find lots of chilly windstorms on the planet. Scientists think these winds roar at speeds of 400 miles an hour! One big storm on the surface of the planet is about the size of Mars.

It takes Neptune, the eighth planet from the Sun, 164 Earth years to orbit the Sun.

The Voyager space probe sent back this picture of Neptune.

Which planet travels farthest from the Sun?

Pluto is the planet that travels farthest from the Sun. It is about 40 times farther from the Sun than the Earth is. It takes 248 Earth years for Pluto to complete one orbit around the Sun.

Pluto's path around the Sun is stretched out like an oval. Because of this odd orbit, Pluto is traveling closer to the Sun between 1979 and 1999 than it has traveled in other years. During that time, Neptune becomes the planet farthest from the Sun.

From Pluto, the Sun would look like a bright star among the other stars. Daylight on Pluto is like twilight here on Earth!

Which is the smallest planet?

Faraway Pluto is the smallest planet in our solar system. Scientists think it is only 930 miles wide—not even half the size of the Earth's Moon! Cold and dark, Pluto is often called a snowball in space!

ASTEROIDS, COMETS, AND METEORS

What are asteroids?

Asteroids are tiny planets in our solar system. There are thousands of them. Most of them have been discovered in the space between Mars and Jupiter. The largest asteroid is less than 500 miles wide. Most asteroids are chunks of rock that are less than one mile wide.

Through a telescope, asteroids look like stars. The word *asteroid* means "like a star."

The largest asteroid, named Ceres, is almost as big as the state of Texas!

Where did asteroids come from?

Scientists think that asteroids were formed the same time as the Earth and Sun. Asteroids are clumps of material that never grew big enough to become planets.

145

What is a comet?

A comet is a large ball of frozen gases, dust, and ice that glows brightly as it approaches the Sun. It travels in a long, cigar-shaped orbit around the Sun. Comets that can be seen without a telescope often have tails of glowing gases streaming out behind them. A comet's tail always points away from the Sun because the strong solar wind coming from the Sun blows the glowing gases backward off the comet.

A comet's tail can be more than a million miles long!

What is Halley's Comet?

Halley's Comet has appeared in our sky every 75 years since at least 240 B.C. In 1910, the Earth passed through the tail of Halley's Comet, but nothing bad happened because of it. In 1985 and 1986, Halley's Comet passed by the Earth again. Scientists from more than 50 countries used new instruments to collect new information. They learned that the nucleus, or head, of Halley's Comet is shaped like a peanut. It is about nine miles long and five miles wide.

Why are some people afraid of comets?

Long ago, people were very frightened by comets. They believed that comets were signs of bad luck—sickness, war, floods, or even the end of the world. They were afraid that a comet would crash into the Earth and destroy it. Today, we accept comets as a part of our solar system. Comets are interesting to scientists because they are made of the same materials from which the planets were formed.

What are meteors?

Meteors (MEE-tee-oars), often called shooting stars, are bright streaks of light speeding through the sky. A meteor appears when a bit of dust or rock that has been traveling through space vaporizes—heats up and turns to gas. The rock vaporizes because of the friction created as it speeds through the Earth's atmosphere. The glowing vapors are the streaks of light you see. A very brilliant meteor that leaves a shining trail as it streaks across the sky is called a fireball. Its trail lasts for as long as a minute or two.

What is a meteor shower?

A meteor shower happens when many meteors fall from the same place in the sky. A meteor shower can last for hours or even a few days. Scientists think the meteors of a meteor shower are millions of tiny pieces of a broken-up comet. These pieces fall into the Earth's air and burn up in it.

What is a meteorite?

A chunk of rock that does not completely burn up as it travels through the Earth's atmosphere is called a meteorite. It falls and lands on Earth.

Most meteorites have fallen in places where no one lives. In the past 100 years, only about 20 to 30 have fallen near people. There is no record that anyone has ever been seriously hurt by one.

A meteorite falling through Earth's atmosphere.

The world's largest meteorite landed in Namibia, Africa. It weighs about 60 tons—as much as nine elephants!

CHAPTER 18

Can stars make your wishes come true? Can you catch a falling star and put it in your pocket? From songs to stories to stargazing, the subject of stars has fascinated people since the beginning of time. What are stars really like? Well, let's go swing among them and we'll find out!

STAR-GAZING

STAR FACTS

What makes the stars shine?

Like our Sun, which is a star, stars shine with their own light because they are very hot. A lot of gases press down, causing great heat at the center of a star, and the star begins to shine.

The heart of a star reaches nearly 30 million degrees Fahrenheit. A grain of sand that hot would kill a person up to 100 miles away!

How big are the stars?

Stars are the biggest balls of gases scientists have found. They come in many sizes. Some stars, called dwarfs, are small—about the size of the Earth. Red dwarfs are small, cool, and faint. White dwarfs are very hot, but they appear faint in the sky because of their small size.

Our Sun is a middle-sized yellow star, more than a million times larger than the Earth. Many other stars are about the same size.

Some stars, called giants and supergiants, are much larger than our Sun. Orange giants and red supergiants are cool stars, but they are very bright, because of their huge size. Blue supergiants are the hottest, brightest stars of all.

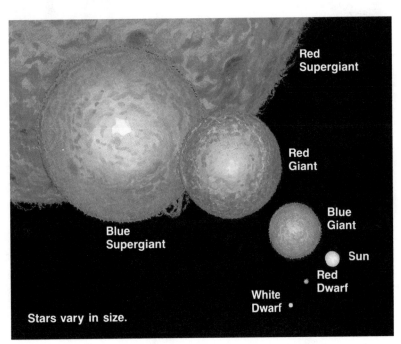

Blue Supergiant

Red Supergiant

Red Giant

Blue Giant

Sun

Red Dwarf

White Dwarf

Stars vary in size.

The biggest supergiants known are 700 times larger than the Sun!

Why are stars different colors?

If you look at stars very carefully through a telescope, you will see that they have different colors. Their colors are caused by their temperature. Although all stars are very hot, some are hotter than others.

The hottest stars that you can see are blue-white. Yellow stars like the Sun are medium-hot. The coolest stars you can see are red.

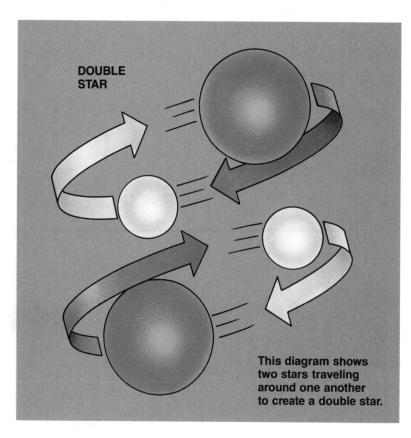

DOUBLE STAR

This diagram shows two stars traveling around one another to create a double star.

Is there such a thing as a double star?

Yes, there are thousands of them. A double star is made up of two neighboring stars that travel around each other. Most double stars look like single stars unless you look at them through a telescope.

One of the most mysterious double stars is called Epsilon Aurigae. These two stars revolve around each other every 27 years. Some scientists think that one star in this pair is the largest star ever known. If this star were placed in the middle of our solar system, its edge would reach as far as Uranus! Because it is so distant, this double star looks no brighter than other stars in the sky.

What is a star cluster?

A star cluster is made up of many stars that travel near each other. One popular star cluster, called Pleiades (PLEE-uh-deez), or the Seven Sisters, has about 400 stars in it. You can easily find this cluster in the night sky during the fall and winter without using a telescope. You will see five or six stars together in a clump. Through binoculars, you will see a dozen or more, and a telescope will show you hundreds!

Why do stars twinkle?

Stars don't really twinkle; they just seem to. There is a thick blanket of air around the Earth. The light coming from the stars must pass through this air. As the starlight passes through, it shifts, or moves about. This happens because of moisture in the air, changing air temperatures, and the constant movement of the air. When we see this shifting starlight, we think the stars are twinkling.

Where do the stars go in the daytime?

They don't go anywhere. They are always in the sky. But the Sun's bright light keeps you from seeing the stars during the day. In the evening, you can begin to see them again.

Stars from Beginning to End

Where do stars come from?

Stars are born from huge clouds of gas and dust known as nebulas. If you traveled through the galaxy, you would sometimes see nebulas floating in the spaces between the stars. Stars begin to grow when a part of a nebula becomes very dense. This dense cloud contracts—gets smaller and hotter—until great heat is created at the center. Then the star begins to shine.

What happens when a star dies out?

During its lifetime, a star continues to contract. Eventually, a star burns up most of its material and begins to die. At first, the dying star begins to lose its gravity. This makes it swell up to an enormous size. Its surface starts to cool, and begins to glow red. At this stage, it is called a red giant.

Hundreds of millions of years may pass before the red giant collapses into a ball about the size of the Earth. This is called a white dwarf star. The white dwarf slowly gives off its last light and burns out. All that's left is a cold, black dwarf star.

Do all stars die out the same way?

Stars larger than our Sun may go through another stage before they die out. After they become red giants, their centers may explode. These great explosions are called supernovas. Supernovas send material flying through space.

What's left of the star becomes a small, dense object. Gravity squeezes the star down until it becomes a neutron star, a star having no electrical charge. It is only a few miles wide.

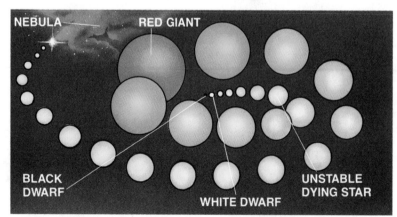

NEBULA   RED GIANT

BLACK DWARF   WHITE DWARF   UNSTABLE DYING STAR

From its beginning as a huge cloud called a nebula to its end as a black dwarf star, a star goes through many phases. This process happens over billions of years.

What is a black hole?

Scientists believe that a black hole is formed when a dying star shrinks beyond the neutron star stage. While the star is burning, its heat and expanding gases help it keep its shape against the force of its own gravity, which is always pulling it inward. As the star cools, its gravity overpowers it, and the whole surface begins to get smaller and smaller.

Eventually, the star has no mass at all. Everything is pulled into its center and becomes invisible. Not even the tiny particles that make up light rays can escape the star's gravity. The star has become a black hole in space.

Will the same stars always be in the sky?

No. Old stars are always dying, and new stars are always being born. Some stars last a few million years. Others go on and on for hundreds of billions of years. But all stars someday either explode or get small and stop shining. At the same time, new stars keep forming from gas and dust in space.

SOMEDAY THIS WILL ALL BE DIFFERENT!

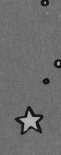

MAPPING OUT THE STARS

How many stars are there in the sky?

On a clear night, you can see about 2,000 stars just by looking up. You could see many thousands more with a small telescope. Giant telescopes allow you to see billions of stars.

As the Earth travels around the Sun, your view of the stars changes. If you stargaze monthly, you may see 6,000 different stars by the year's end.

Scientists keep building larger telescopes, enabling them to see farther into space. With each new telescope, scientists discover more stars. Some stars were too dim or too far away to show up in smaller telescopes. Since new stars are always being discovered, no one knows how many stars really exist.

What is the Big Dipper?

The Big Dipper is a group of stars in the sky. If you could draw a line to connect them, you'd see that they look like the cup and handle of a water dipper.

Mizar (MY-zahr), the star at the bend of the Big Dipper's handle, is a double star. With a telescope, you can see its dim companion star.

The Big Dipper is one of many groups of stars that people have named for their shapes. We call these groups constellations (kon-stuh-LAY-shunz).

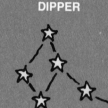

LITTLE DIPPER

BIG DIPPER

IF WE COULD JUST FIND THE NORTH STAR, WE COULD FIND OUR WAY HOME.

What are the names of some other constellations?

You may have heard of the constellations Orion, the Hunter; Pegasus, the Winged Horse; or Ursa Major, the Great Bear.

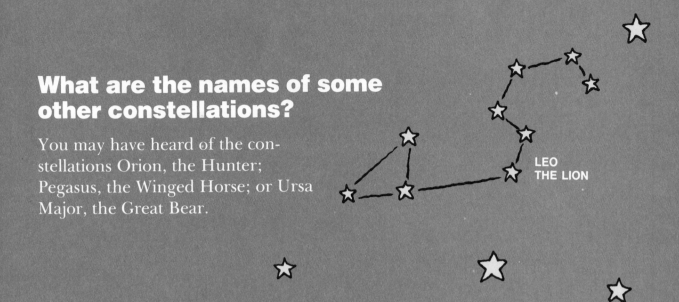

LEO
THE LION

NORTH STAR

IT MIGHT BE EASIER, IF THEY'D JUST USE MY MAP.

How can the stars help you if you are lost at night?

One very important star—the North Star—can help you, even though it's not the brightest star in the sky. You can find the North Star easily. The two stars in front of the Big Dipper point to it. If you face the North Star, you are facing north.

Some people learn the locations of other constellations to find the other directions. For example, in the winter, Orion, the Hunter, shows us the south. In the spring, Leo, the Lion, will be in the south, and this is where you find Scorpius in the summer. Stargazers can have fun finding the constellations and figuring out the directions.

I'VE ALWAYS THOUGHT "SNOOPY" MEANT "GREAT DOG."

• After the Sun, the next-brightest star in our sky is Sirius, the Dog Star. It has that name because it is in the group of stars called Canis Major, which means Great Dog.

• Since 1974, a radio message beamed from the Arecibo radio telescope in Puerto Rico has been racing toward a cluster of stars called M13. Will there be creatures on M13 to receive and understand the message? Only time will tell, but if any creatures do receive our message and answer right away, the reply will come about 50,000 years from the time the message was sent. If anyone here is still listening!

• There is a kind of telescope, called a radio telescope, that can find stars even in the daytime! It picks up radio waves that come from outer space, the way your radio at home picks up radio waves from a station many miles away. All stars and some planets give off these waves. So do other faraway objects, such as galaxies and quasars. By listening to radio waves, scientists learn more about everything in outer space.

YES, MA'AM.

THIS IS MY REPORT ON QUASARS.

SOME ARE 58,800,000 TRILLION MILES AWAY!

AND I JUST LEARNED TO COUNT TO 100!

• Some scientists believe that the universe is expanding—getting bigger. They don't know how and why it's happening, but when they study the light from distant stars, they can see that other galaxies are racing away from ours.

Some scientists expect the universe to go on as it is for billions of years. After that, they think the last stars will shine and go out. The universe will become dark and cold.

Other scientists think that gravity will keep the galaxies from moving apart. They think the galaxies will fall together to form a glob of matter. This glob will explode in another big bang, and a new universe will begin!

• In 1963, radio waves were discovered coming from objects that look like bright stars but shine brighter than the brightest galaxies! What could they be? Scientists named these waves quasars. Quasars might be the earliest stages in the life of a galaxy. About 1,300 quasars have been discovered. They are the most distant objects that we can see. Some are 58,800,000 trillion miles away. That's 58,800,000,000,-000,000,000!

HOW LONG UNTIL THE NEXT BIG BANG?

There's much more to discover in Snoopy's World.
If you've enjoyed *Land and Space*,
you'll want to read...

How Things Work

People and Customs of the World

Earth, Water and Air

Creatures, Large and Small